Building Phonemic Awareness And Early Reading Skills

By

Barbara Gruber, M.A. Ed.

Helene Chirinian, M.A. Ed.

Editor

Amy Erickson

Copy Editors

Laurel Robinson

Debbie Shoffner

Gina Sutphin

Artist

Marilynn G. Barr

Manufactured in the United States

10 9 8 7 6 5 4 3 2 1

Table Of Contents

Questions And Answers

Kindergarten teachers have the awesome responsibility of launching students' school careers. Perhaps no aspect of teaching little learners is more rewarding than preparing them for the adventure of lifelong reading.

This book is brimming with teaching strategies and educational activities designed to strengthen your reading program and foster students' love of literature. These ready-to-use ideas are educationally sound and developmentally appropriate, and they require little preparation—just what busy, dedicated teachers need!

What makes this book different from other reading books?

This book is unique because it addresses both phonics and phonemic awareness. Phonemic awareness is the foundation upon which phonics skills are based, and it is an essential component of successful reading programs.

Aren't phonemic awareness and phonics the same?

Phonemic awareness is the understanding that oral language is composed of a series of sounds. Phonics, however, is the relationship between oral and written language—translating sounds into print. Phonemic awareness is critical to the long-term effectiveness of phonics programs. Phonemic awareness activities explore and manipulate sounds. These activities should be presented in a general progression. However, the stages of phonemic awareness are not mutually exclusive. The phonemic awareness skill areas (rhyming, alliteration, comparing and contrasting, blending, segmenting, and manipulating sounds) complement each other and can be woven together in lessons.

But what about my current program?

This book is designed to supplement, not replace, your current phonics program, and it can be used in conjunction with any reading program. This book explains how to
- establish a print-rich environment;
- create, organize, and use a variety of teaching tools;
- involve parents in your educational program;
- use literature to target skills;
- develop phonemic awareness;
- teach letter recognition and sounds; and
- prepare students for the transition to first grade.

About This Book

Where does literature fit into phonemic awareness and phonics?

Everywhere! Literature is an integral part of successful reading programs. Students need to be exposed to high-quality literature right from the start. Students need to learn that sounds are related to print and that print has meaning. Using literature to address phonemic awareness and phonics skills is very effective. This book recommends some wonderful titles and suggests ways to reinforce skills with literature. With your modeling, students will also acquire concepts about print, such as directionality and one-to-one correspondence between oral and written words. Even more important, they will be excited about reading!

What about writing?
When should I introduce it to my students?

Right away! Even the youngest of children are eager to imitate adults writing grocery lists, letters, or notes. By watching adults in their environment, youngsters learn that written symbols have meaning. Reading and writing are interrelated skills. This book provides activities and suggestions for establishing a print-rich environment that facilitates the development of both reading and writing. You'll also find ideas for publishing student work in the section titled "The Reading And Writing Connection." With these tips and activities, you'll be well on the way to launching a successful reading program!

Setting The Stage!

Your Classroom Environment

The first step to assure phonics and reading success is to establish the right environment. Classroom settings have the potential to motivate and engage students in exciting learning experiences. They can also convey a warm and inviting tone to visitors. Above all, the settings can and should send the message that children and learning are valued. Try these appealing ideas to establish a print-rich classroom that promotes literacy.

Rain Gutter Book Holders

Before making this unique book holder, check with the school administrator to see if you may attach a rain gutter section to your classroom wall. To make this book holder, purchase a section of rain gutter from your local building-supply store. Rain gutters are sold in metal or plastic ten-foot sections. You may want to buy end caps as well to prevent books from sliding off the display. Ask the school custodian to help you attach the rain gutter to the wall. (The space below the chalk ledge is a good level for children.) Place the books that you'd like to feature in the resulting book holder. It will accommodate books of nearly any size, and the covers will be visible to young readers at a glance. Rain or shine, these handy holders will please you and your students!

Library Lure

Entice students to check out the classroom library by making it a focal point in your room. Display colorful posters, banners, and mobiles promoting literature. Provide comfortable seating with carpet squares, a rocker or an overstuffed chair, and beanbag chairs. Station several puppets and stuffed animals in the library to make it even more inviting. Display as many books as possible with the covers visible to students. No doubt the library will be the number one attraction in your classroom!

Book Commercials

Channel students' attention to featured books with commercials. At a pre-determined time each day, select a book to advertise, and tell students about the unique aspects of the book. Be sure to highlight the cover, illustrations, and a portion of the text in your commercial. Then place the book in a "Special Book Of The Day" exhibit. The next day, add this book to the classroom library and choose a different book to promote. Students will be eager to check out the advertised "specials"!

Connecting Literacy And Centers

Incorporate these engaging ideas into your centers to capture students' interest and to promote literacy.

- **Reading Center**
  Bears: Create a den with a large cardboard box and paint. It will make a perfect hideaway for young readers.
  Picnic: Spread a red and white checkered tablecloth on your classroom library floor, and pack tempting books in a large picnic basket.
  Farm: Create a cozy reading area by making a barn with a large cardboard box. Add a bale of hay for a look of authenticity.
  Summer Fun: A small inflatable wading pool makes a great place to relax and read. Don't forget a supply of beach towels!
  Circus: Decorate the classroom library with balloons and streamers. Provide clown hats for students to wear when they read.

- **Writing Center**
  As you know, it's important for each student to work at his level, whether it is drawing, scribbling, or writing letter strings. Provide opportunities for students to experiment with their developing writing skills with a variety of writing materials, such as discarded greeting cards, stencils, assorted paper, decorative notepads, blank books, pens, and colored pencils.

- **Dramatic Play**
  Restaurant: Supply small notepads for writing orders. Copies of take-out menus would also be great additions to the center.
  Grocery Store: Gather a supply of empty cracker, cereal, and cookie boxes. Youngster will love to read them as they "shop." Provide small notepads for writing lists, too.
  Shoe, Toy, Or Pet Stores: Have large strips of paper and small index cards available for students to make store signs and price tags. Catalogues would also be useful materials.

- **Blocks**
  Provide paper, pencils, and crayons for students to label their buildings and to make road signs.

- **Science**
  Station science logs in this center for students to write and draw about your class pet, plants, or science experiments.

- **Art**
  Place a variety of paper strips and cards for students to use in creating artwork labels and signs.

You've seen in your own classroom that children learn more by doing than by watching. As active engagement increases, management problems decrease and learning increases. Teaching tools that interest and involve every student can be inexpensive and require little, if any, preparation time. Having a wealth of organizational ideas at your fingertips ensures that the tools you need will be easily accessible and convenient. Be sure to add these tricks of the trade to your teacher's toolbox!

Write On!

Provide each student with chalk, an individual chalkboard, and a sock. Then have him respond to a question or direction by writing on his chalkboard. You may, for example, ask each student to write a specific letter. At a predetermined signal, ask each student to hold up his chalkboard for you to see. At a glance, you'll be able to tell which students understand a concept and which need more practice. Have each student use a sock to erase his chalkboard and put his chalk in the sock's toe for easy storage.

Smile While You Work

Elicit responses from all of your students with a smile. Cut a five-inch circle from poster board for each student in your class. Draw a happy face on one side and a sad face on the other. Ask students to use their happy/sad faces for activities that require yes/no responses. Upon request, have each student show a happy face to indicate yes or a sad face for no. Your students will be all smiles with this approach to active engagement!

Magnetic Surfaces

Looking for surfaces where magnetic letters can be used and displayed? If so, try magnetic cookie trays or burner covers. They are inexpensive and just the right size for little hands!

Dozens Of Letters

You probably have batches of alphabet manipulatives in your classroom. Lots of loose pieces are an organizational headache when you prepare and teach language arts lessons. Here's a solution! Obtain a 12-serving-size muffin pan. Use masking tape and a marker to label each cup with two or three letters in alphabetical order. Place magnetic, foam, or tile letters in the corresponding cups. Not only will each letter be easy to find when you need it, but students' matching and ABC skills will be reinforced as well.

Organizational Ideas

Tips For Pointers

When reading charts and big books, use captivating pointers to spark students' interest and increase attention to print. Here are a few ideas for creating pointers:

- Wooden spoon: Use with a recipe chart or a story about food.
- Magic wand: Perfect for fairy tales. (If a store-bought one isn't readily available, one can easily be made with a cardboard tube or dowel, paint, and glitter.)
- Versatile pointer: For a pointer that can be used with any topic, tape a thematic poster-board cutout to the tip of a dowel.

Hoops Of Fun

Try this idea for ABC sorting in a jiffy. Place two Hula-Hoops® beside each other on the classroom floor. Label two index cards with the categories that will be addressed in the activity, such as words that begin with /b/ and those that begin with /m/. Place each index card in front of a hoop, and have students place picture cards or small objects into the appropriate hoops. Students can clearly distinguish between the two sets, and the hoops can be quickly emptied and prepared for a different sorting lesson.

Morning Message Memory Book

Keep those morning messages! Instead of discarding or erasing your daily messages, save them and use them as a teaching tool throughout the year. Emphasize a skill, such as uppercase letters, as you record your morning message on a small chart tablet. Then ask a student to illustrate the message. The next day, review the previous day's message and then turn the page to write a new one. Continue in this manner until the tablet is full. Cover the front of the tablet with decorative Con-Tact® paper and use a permanent marker to add a title. Display the book in a special section of the classroom library for students to enjoy again and again.

Pocket Charts

As you know, a pocket chart is a great management tool for centers, classroom jobs, and a variety of other classroom routines. A pocket chart is also an invaluable tool for teachers of developing readers. It is a highly effective context for shared reading with groups of kindergarten students.

Benefits Of Shared Reading With
Pocket Charts In Kindergarten

- The whole group can see the pocket chart as the teacher models fluency and expression.

- Pocket charts give students the opportunity to manipulate print in a concrete manner, allowing them to make choices and develop a sense of autonomy and ownership.

- Shared reading connects spoken and written language.

- All students can participate in a noncompetitive and supportive environment in which they can be successful.

- Children's comfort level with text increases and they become more confident.

- Youngsters learn the conventions of print, such as tracking from left to right, letters, words, and sentences.

- The reading material is easily made available for students to revisit and practice independently.

- Students gain sound-symbol knowledge and increase their sight-word vocabularies. With repeated shared readings, children develop fluency.

- Reading together is fun. Shared reading fosters a love of literature!

Hickory Dickory Dock.
The mouse ran up the clock!
The clock struck one.
The mouse ran down.
Hickory Dickory Dock.

Build-A-Word Cards

As you plan ahead for phonics lessons, you may want to prepare individual student sets of Build-A-Word cards as well as a teacher set. Specific ideas for using these cards are provided in the phonics section of this book. These easy-to-make cards will be one of the most useful tools in your classroom. Each child manipulates his own cards during phonics lessons and is actively engaged in the learning process. At a glance, you'll be able to check students' comprehension of the concepts you're teaching.

Teacher Card Set

This set of cards is perfect for whole-group instruction. You can display them on the chalkboard ledge or on an easel. They are also easy for you and the students to hold and manipulate during individual or small group activities. To make a set of cards, duplicate on tagboard 26 copies of the "Teacher Build-A-Word Card Patterns" on page 17. Using a thick black marker, print each upper and lowercase letter on a separate card. If desired, highlight the vowels to alert students to these special letters. Create extra cards of commonly used letters as needed. Laminate the cards for durability before cutting them apart.

Student Card Sets

This set of cards provides easy-to-manipulate letters for children to use at their desks as you model letters and words with your set of large cards. A dot below each letter helps students correctly orient their letter cards. For each child in your class, duplicate a set of "Student Build-A-Word Cards" (pages 12–16) on white construction paper. If desired, highlight the vowels. Create extra cards of commonly used letters as needed. Laminate the cards for durability, then cut them apart.

Directions To Make A Card Holder:

1. Hold a sheet of 9" x 12" heavy paper as shown. (Laminate it before use to increase durability if desired.)
2. Mark each side $2\frac{1}{2}$" and 4" from the bottom edge.
3. Make a fold at the $2\frac{1}{2}$" marks.
4. Place the fold at the 4" marks to create a $\frac{3}{4}$"-deep pocket.
5. Staple the pocket at each side.

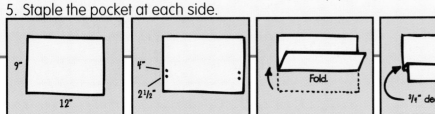

Finished size:
$7\frac{1}{2}$" x 12"

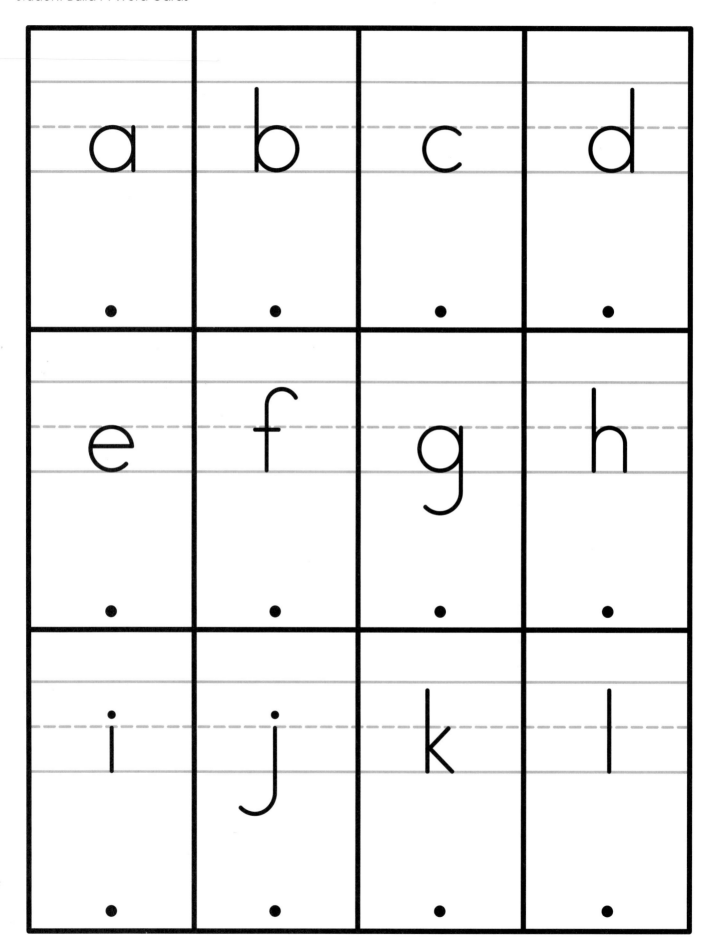

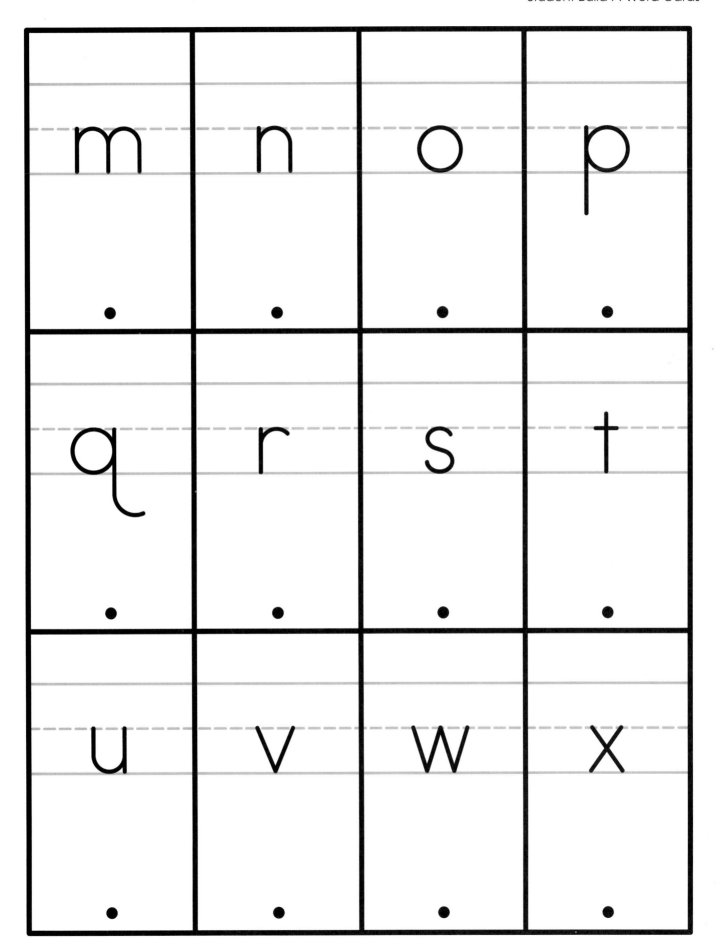

m	n	o	p
q	r	s	t
u	v	w	x

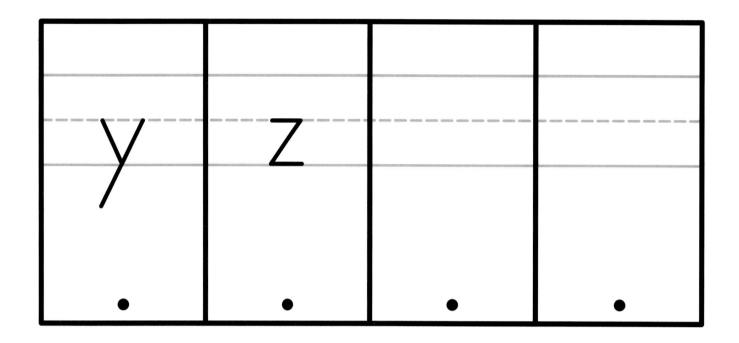

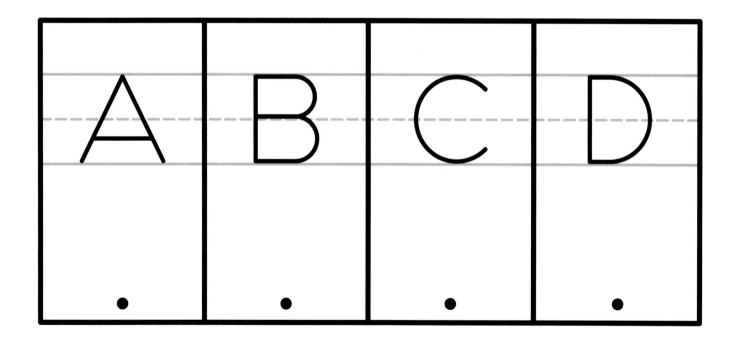

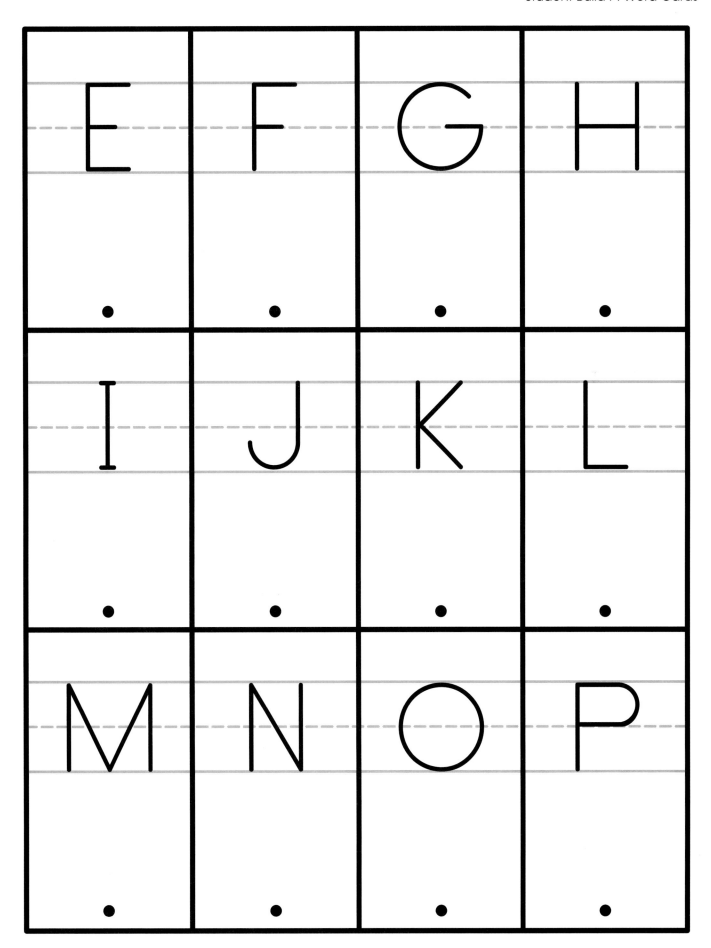

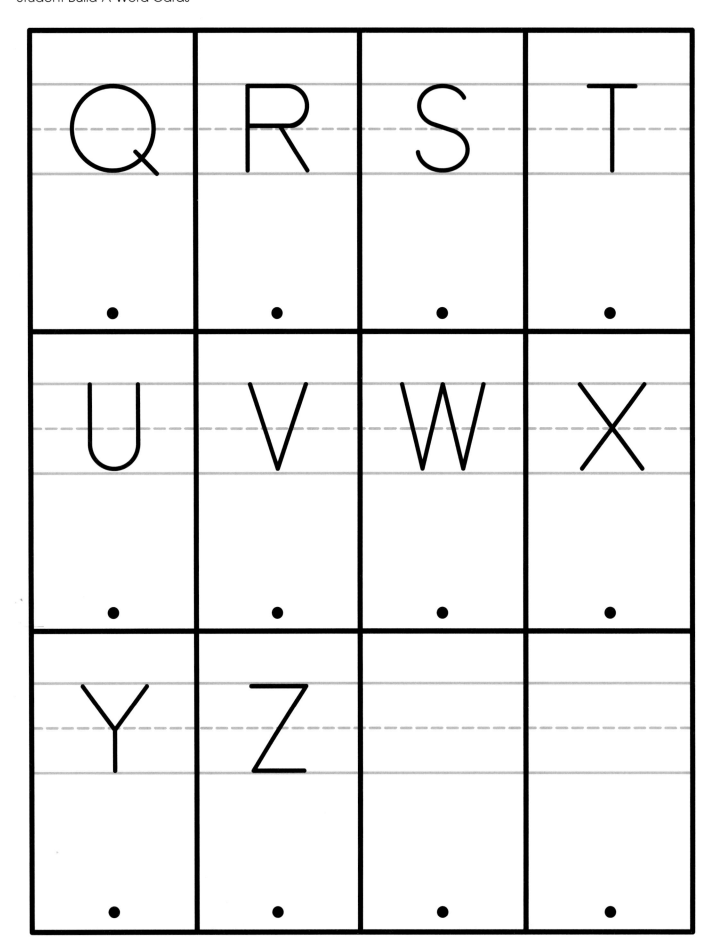

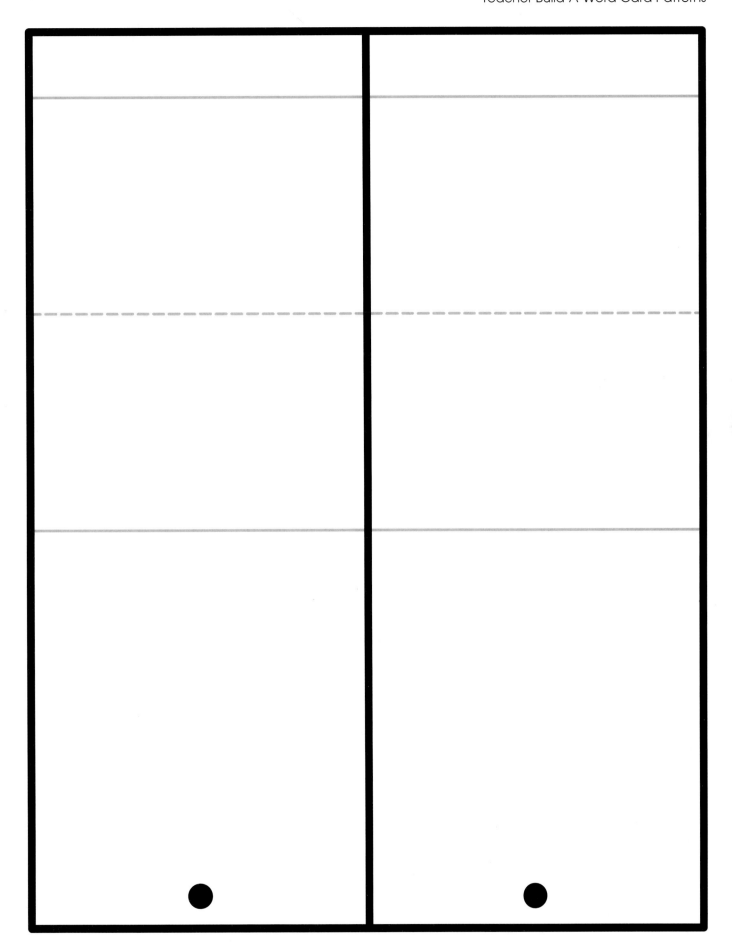

Home-School Connections

Parent* involvement in educational programs can make a significant and positive impact on students' achievement. Parents can support the learning process both at home and at school. Here are some suggestions for promoting parent involvement, specifically in your reading and writing programs.

Welcome parents in the classroom.

- Host an Open House at the beginning of the year. Present an overview of your reading program. Show sample reading materials and model how to share literature with young children.
- Periodically invite parents to presentations of the poems, songs, and charts that your youngsters have learned. Incorporate movements, picture cards, puppets, and other props.
- Schedule times that parents may observe phonics or other types of lessons.
- Invite parents to be guest readers.

Keep parents informed.

- Send home class newsletters regularly. Describe recent classroom activities, suggest how families can promote a positive attitude toward reading, and provide ideas to reinforce skills at home.
- Describe expected kindergarten milestones.
- Explain assessment tools.

Enlist volunteers.

- Provide materials for volunteers to prepare at home. Some parents' schedules do not allow for them to help during the day. Other parents might simply be more comfortable helping at home than at school.
- Arrange for volunteers to practice specific skills with students. Establish a tutoring center in the classroom for work with individual students.
- Ask volunteers to help prepare and organize teaching materials.
- Coordinate a volunteer publishing center. (Specific ideas about how to do so are found on pages 20–21.)
- Have volunteers read aloud to students. Reading aloud to students is one of the most powerful ways to increase reading achievement!

*Please note that for the purposes of this text, "parent" refers to a child's primary caregiver. However, these suggestions are also appropriate for other adults in a child's life who would like to be actively involved in his education.

Teacher-Parent Connection

Dear Parents,

Help your child develop a lifelong love for reading and learning with these ideas.

- Establish a special family reading time, and read aloud to your child every day. Continue having read-aloud times even after your child can read independently.

- Read simple, predictable stories and encourage your child to chime in with you.

- Reread favorite books again and again. Rereading helps children develop confidence and fluency.

- Sit side by side and point to the text as you read.

- Help your child get a card for the public library, and plan regular visits.

- Read one of your own books silently as your child looks at books and reads independently. Even though your child is reading by himself, the fact that you're in the same room reading gives him the message that reading is important.

- Write to your child. Leave brief messages for him in his lunchbox or under his pillow.

- Point out times that you read and write throughout the day, such as when you read recipes, make grocery lists, read the newspaper, and read street signs.

Share the joy of reading and learning with your child!

Sincerely,

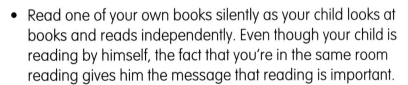
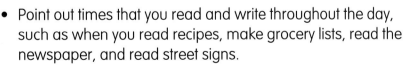

The Reading And Writing Connection

As you've observed children, you've noticed that reading and writing are interrelated processes. Writing requires an understanding of the sounds of language (phonemic awareness) and how they translate into print (phonics)—the very core of reading. To help youngsters move from the scribbling and drawing stage of writing to using phonetic skills, it's important to provide them with as many opportunities to read and write as possible. One very effective method of doing that is publishing student-written books.

Books written by either individual students or by the entire class are powerful motivators for both reading and writing. Students are proud to see their writing in published form, and the familiar text enables them to experience success as readers. Capitalize on the positive influence of publishing student-made books and establish a publishing center in your classroom, or explore the possibility of creating a grade-level or schoolwide publishing center. The more people and resources involved, the greater impact your endeavor will have.

Publishing Center Considerations

There are countless ways to establish and manage a publishing center. Here are some things to think about when you are planning one.

- **Time:** A publishing center can be a time-consuming element in your classroom. One very simple and effective way to address this issue is having parent volunteers help organize and run the center.

- **Training:** You may want to train one or two volunteers, and then have them assume the responsibility for training other volunteers. If you plan to publish student work on a computer, additional training may be needed. Make your expectations clear to the volunteers, and post a set of written guidelines in the center. Explain how you would like volunteers to provide feedback to students and how you would like the finished books to look.

- **Preparation:** Make an assortment of blank books in advance (sample ideas follow on pages 21–23), and replenish the supply as needed. Some volunteers may be interested in making books during periodic after-school sessions, at home, or in the classroom on a regular basis.

- **Materials:** Keep a variety of publishing materials accessible. These may include wallpaper, heavy paper, duplicating paper, loose-leaf rings, staplers, hole punchers, adhesive labels (for titles), dictionaries (to check spelling), and writing and drawing supplies.

- **Management:** Decide on a record-keeping system. Determine a method that does not interfere with the flow of your class and will let volunteers know which students are ready to publish. Perhaps a simple checklist on a clipboard in the center will meet your needs.

- **Recognition:** Determine how you will showcase students' work. Will you designate a special place in the classroom library for student-written books? Will some books be donated to the school library? Perhaps you would like to schedule an end-of-the-year authors' celebration and invite parents, friends, and staff members to listen to students read their books.

Constructing Books

Class Books

One of the simplest ways to make a class book is to choose a familiar topic and brainstorm related ideas with students. Then have each child choose an idea to illustrate on a sheet of paper. (You may want to fold under the bottom edge of their papers to save adequate space for their text.) While students are working, circulate and have each one dictate a caption while you write it below his picture. Make a cover and laminate it for durability if desired. Compile the pages and cover; then bind them together with staples, loose-leaf rings, or with hand stitching. A plastic spiral binding machine is another good binding tool. At the end of the school year, hold a drawing and give the class books to students for special end-of-the-year mementos.

Basic Individual Book

Simply fold the desired number of duplicating sheets in half. Fold a slightly larger piece of construction paper in half and slip the folded pages between the resulting cover. To bind the book, staple on the fold, or hole-punch two holes on the left edge and thread yarn through the holes and tie it. Wallpaper and tagboard are great alternatives to construction paper and they add variety, too.

Step Booklet

Stack three 8½" x 11" sheets of white paper and hold the pages vertically in front of you. Slide the top sheet upward approximately one inch; then repeat the process for the second sheet. Next fold the paper thicknesses forward to create six graduated pages as shown. Staple close to the fold.

Box Book

Cut the front and back from an empty cereal box to make a cover for a story about favorite breakfast foods. Slip the story pages between the covers, hole-punch the resulting book along the left edge, and fasten with loose-leaf rings.

Important Pages To Include In Student-Created Books

- Title page with title, author, illustrator, publisher, and publication date
- Dedication page
- About The Author page (A self-portrait or small photo adds a nice touch to this page.)

Accordion Book

Fold a long sheet of paper in half lengthwise (12" x 36" bulletin-board paper works well). Fold the paper accordion-style into equal parts. Glue a piece of tagboard inside each end section for durability. Glue story pages onto each section and decorate the covers as desired.

Calendar Book

Calendars focus on many themes that are perfect for kindergarten class books. Ask friends and students' families to donate their calendars to your class at the end of the year. Here are two ways to make books from calendars:

Method 1: Cut the pictures from a calendar and place them in a magnetic photo album. Have students dictate a sentence for each picture. Record the sentences on strips of paper and add them to the pages.

Method 2: Simply paste a sheet of heavy paper over each calendar grid. Then write students' sentences directly on the paper, or glue a separate sheet of duplicating paper with the text onto the heavy paper. The pages of this unique book open from bottom to top!

Topics For Student-Written Books

Class Books

- Our Yummy In The Tummy Book (favorite foods)
- Summer Memories
- Animal ABC Book
- When It Rains…
- Our Weekend Fun Book
- At School
- All About Our Field Trip

Basic Individual Books

- My Family
- All About Me
- My Favorite Stuffed Animal
- Vacation Time
- My Pets

Step Books

- Colors
- Seasons
- Number Concepts
- Steps summarizing a class project or recipe

Accordion Books

- Parts of the school day
- Retelling a story (summarizing and sequencing main events)
- Student information book (e.g., name, birthday, address, telephone number)

Materials And Techniques For Illustrating Books And Decorating Covers

- rubber stamps
- sponge-painting
- photographs
- stencils and cutouts
- pictures from discarded magazines and greeting cards
- fingerpainting
- tissue-paper or wallpaper collages
- leaf rubbings
- potato and apple prints

Learning About Print

Basic knowledge about print—such as the understanding that text is read from top to bottom and from left to right—forms the foundation for reading skills. To increase students' print awareness, you want to provide a classroom that is rich with functional, meaningful, and engaging print. Your classroom schedules, job charts, coat hook labels, big books, and pocket charts are some of the materials that help you teach children about print. As you read aloud with these materials, point to each word and invite children to read along with you. Elicit student participation by having students accompany your reading with movements, take turns using a pointer to track the print, and make predictions about stories. With repeated readings, students will develop concepts about print as well as sight-word vocabularies.

These are some of the print concepts that youngsters need to develop in order to become successful readers:

- Understanding that print holds meaning
- Correct orientation of books
- Beginning of a sentence
- Word-print match
- Directionality and return sweep
- Upper- and lowercase letters and letter names

Pocket Chart Ideas
To Develop Print Awareness

Experience Chart

Discuss a recent class field trip, event, or project with your students and have them dictate a story about it. Write each sentence on a separate sentence strip, sequence the strips in the pocket chart, and read them aloud together. Ask students to determine a title for the story, add it to the chart, and then reread the story several times.

Variations:
- Have students illustrate each sentence on an index card and place the cards into the corresponding pockets.
- Add photos to illustrate the story.
- After adding picture clues, scramble the sentences and have students sequence them.
- For a challenging task after several readings, select a few words to reinforce and write them on separate cards. Have students match them with the original text.

Calendar And Weather
Pocket Chart

Incorporate the pocket chart shown into your daily routine. Add stencil cutouts or stickers to correspond with the weather words. Display a flannelboard figure beside the chart for students to outfit according to the weather. Enlist students' help in changing the words and pictures. Ask student volunteers to use a pointer to lead the group in reading the chart.

Good Morning, Readers!
Today is Monday.
The month is September.
The date is September 10.
It is a cold and windy day.

Learning About Print

Birthday Chart

Commemorate each child's birthday with this pocket chart. Feature students who have summer birthdays during the last few weeks of the school year.

Make separate cards for each child's name, the numerals 1-6, and the words "he" and "she." Write the children's names and ages in colors that are different from the rest of the text. Use Velcro® or tape to attach paper or store-bought candles to cake cutouts to correspond with students' ages.

Happy Birthday to you!
Today is Carter's birthday.
He is 6 years old.
We make a cake.
Mix, stir, shake, bake.
How many candles does it take?
1, 2, 3, 4, 5, 6
Happy Birthday!

Nursery rhymes, songs, jump rope chants, and poems are perfect for pocket charts, too!

Poetry Books And Big Books

Enjoy these predictable and engaging literature selections with your students to increase their awareness of print.

Poetry

Hand Rhymes
Collected and illustrated by Marc Brown (Puffin Books, 1993)

Read-Aloud Rhymes For The Very Young
Selected by Jack Prelutsky and illustrated by Marc Brown (Alfred A. Knopf Books For Young Readers, 1986)

Big Books

Don't Forget The Bacon!
Written and illustrated by Pat Hutchins (William Morrow And Company, Inc.; 1994)

Rosie's Walk
Written and illustrated by Pat Hutchins (Scholastic Inc., 1992)

Polar Bear, Polar Bear, What Do You Hear?
Written by Bill Martin, Jr., and illustrated by Eric Carle (Henry Holt And Company, Inc.; 1992)

If You Give A Moose A Muffin
Written by Laura Joffe Numeroff and illustrated by Felicia Bond (HarperCollins Children's Books, 1994)

If You Give A Mouse A Cookie
Written by Laura Joffe Numeroff and illustrated by Felicia Bond (HarperCollins Children's Books, 1996)

Chicken Soup With Rice
by Maurice Sendak (Scholastic Inc., 1992)

Shoes
Written by Elizabeth Winthrop and illustrated by William Joyce (HarperCollins Children's Books, 1993)

The Napping House
Written by Audrey Wood and illustrated by Don Wood (Harcourt Brace & Company, 1991)

Phonemic Awareness

What is phonemic awareness?

Phonemic awareness is the understanding that words are composed of a series of sounds. Phonemic awareness activities are usually oral. They engage learners in manipulating sounds and exploring language. Phonemic awareness prepares students for phonics instruction, but it is not related to print or letter names. Phonics activities, on the other hand, are associated with print and focus on the relationship between sounds and letters.

Why is it important to include phonemic awareness in my program?

Phonemic awareness is necessary for success with phonics, spelling, and word recognition. A language-rich environment that exposes children to good literature and frequent opportunities to write facilitates development of phonemic awareness. Children do not usually acquire phonemic awareness without direct instruction.

How can I possibly add phonemic awareness to my already-full curriculum?

Phonemic awareness activities need not adversely impact your busy and demanding classroom schedule. These activities should be brief and can be effectively woven into many daily language activities that you already do.

What types of phonemic awareness activities are appropriate for my students?

The phonemic awareness tasks described on the following page vary in degree of difficulty. They are presented as a continuum from those that are usually easiest for learners to those that are typically more challenging. It is not necessary, however, for students to achieve mastery with one type of task before moving to the next. More than one task can be addressed during a single lesson. Students should have experience with the first four types of tasks before the end of kindergarten. The fifth type is included for those kindergartners who are ready for more complex reading tasks.

Phonemic Awareness

Phonemic Awareness Tasks

1. **Rhyming And Alliteration**
Students identify and produce rhymes and alliteration.
Sample activity: Read aloud a nursery rhyme and have students identify the rhyming words.

2. **Oddity**
Students compare and contrast beginning, middle, or final sounds.
Sample activity: Say "cat, pig, coat" and ask students which of the words begins with a different sound.

3. **Blending**
Say the sounds (phonemes) of a word and have students put them together to form the word.
Sample activity: Tell students to listen to the following sounds and have them blend the phonemes to make a word: /d/ /u/ /k/.

4. **Segmenting**
Students break down words into phonemes. Students may also be asked to count or tap phonemes.
Sample activity: Ask students to identify the number of sounds in the word hat.

5. **Manipulating**
Students manipulate (remove, replace, reorder) the phonemes of a word.
Sample activity: Have students say "bat." Ask them to say it again without saying /b/.

Rhyming

Literature Selections For Rhyming Skills

Read aloud literature with rhyming text to capture students' interest and build phonemic awareness. Playful literature delights youngsters so they are eager to hear the stories again and again. When children chime in as favorite rhyming stories are shared, youngsters experience success as readers. Here are a few popular selections to facilitate students' development of rhyming skills in context.

Skill: Identify rhyming words
Context: Jesse Bear, What Will You Wear?
Written by Nancy White Carlstrom and illustrated by Bruce Degen (Simon & Schuster Children's Division, 1996)

This singsong text written in question-and-answer format summarizes Jesse's carefree day from morning to night. Jesse's happy-go-lucky nature is clearly evident in the detailed illustrations that show how his wardrobe changes throughout the day.

Read the title to students and ask them to identify the words that rhyme. Explain that this story has many rhyming words, and encourage students to listen for them carefully as you read it aloud. After sharing the story, ask students to identify some of the rhymes that they heard. Then reread the story slowly, and ask the students to give a thumbs-up signal each time they hear a pair of rhyming words. At such times, stop reading and ask students to identify the rhymes that they noticed. This lesson earns two thumbs up for facilitating active student participation!

Skill: Identify and produce rhyming words
Context: Silly Sally
Written and illustrated by Audrey Wood (Harcourt Brace & Company, 1994)

Silly Sally and her acquaintances make their way toward town in a decidedly unique fashion—upside down! The simple, rollicking text and comical illustrations are sure to delight youngsters and tickle their funny bones.

After sharing the story once, reread it slowly, encouraging children to chime in with the rhyming words. Then ask students to identify each character that Sally met and the corresponding rhyme, using the illustrations for clues. Next have students brainstorm other characters Sally might have met and rhyming words to go with them. Record students' ideas with simple picture clues on chart paper. Direct each student to choose an idea from the list and draw an illustration to match on a large sheet of paper. Label each student's paper with the appropriate rhyming words, and mount the completed pictures on a brightly colored bulletin board titled "Silly Sally's Pals."

Jesse Bear, what will you wear?

duck in a truck

Ryming

Literature Selections For Rhyming Skills

Skill: Identify and produce rhyming words
Context: I Was Walking Down The Road
Written by Sarah E. Barchas and illustrated by Jack Kent (Scholastic Inc., 1993)

As a young girl goes about her day, she encounters a variety of creatures, such as a frog jumping on a log and a snail near the mail. She puts each of them in a separate cage. After looking at her large and eclectic ensemble, she decides to set all of the creatures free.

Share this simple, predictable story with your students and encourage them to join in with you as you read. Then have students recall each of the creatures in the story and the matching rhyming phrases. Invite students to imagine that they went on a similar walk. Have youngsters generate an original list of creatures that they might have seen. Record the list on chart paper. Ask students if they can add matching rhyming words. Write these ideas on the chart paper as well. Direct each student to select a creature from the list. Have the student illustrate it on a large sheet of drawing paper. Using the sentence pattern as a model, write appropriate text on each student's page. To make a cover, write the title "Our Class Was Walking Down The Road" on another sheet of paper. Compile the pages and bind them into a unique class book. No doubt students will love to relive their imaginary walk with repeated readings.

Skill: Identify and produce rhyming words
Context: Itchy, Itchy Chicken Pox
Written by Grace Maccarone and illustrated by Betsy Lewin (Scholastic Inc., 1992)

Many youngsters will be able to relate all too readily to the main character of this story. This boy is plagued by itchy, itchy chicken pox and tries in vain to find relief from them until one day, they finally disappear on their own.

After reading aloud this engaging book, reread it again slowly, stopping after each set of pages. Ask students to identify the rhyming words. Then challenge students to identify things in the classroom that rhyme with these words. Continue in the same manner for the remaining pages. Your students will surely be itching to share their rhymes!

29

Rhyming

Literature For Developing Rhyming Skills

Each Peach Pear Plum
Written and illustrated by Janet and Allan Ahlberg (Puffin Books, 1986)

Better Not Get Wet, Jesse Bear
Written by Nancy White Carlstrom and illustrated by Bruce Degen (Simon & Schuster Children's Division, 1988)

The Foot Book
Written and illustrated by Dr. Seuss (Random House Books For Young Readers, 1968)

There's A Wocket In My Pocket!
Written and illustrated by Dr. Seuss (Random House Books For Young Readers, 1974)

In The Tall, Tall Grass
by Denise Fleming (Henry Holt And Company, Inc.; 1995)

More Spaghetti, I Say!
Written by Rita Golden Gelman and illustrated by Mort Gerberg (Scholastic, Inc. 1993)

Is Your Mama A Llama?
Written by Deborah Guarino and illustrated by Steven Kellogg (Scholastic Inc., 1997)

The Day The Goose Got Loose
Written by Reeve Lindbergh and illustrated by Steven Kellogg (Puffin Books, 1995)

To Market, To Market
Written by Anne Miranda and illustrated by Janet Stevens (Harcourt Brace & Company, 1997)

Sheep In A Jeep
Written by Nancy Shaw and illustrated by Margot Apple (Houghton Mifflin Company, 1997)

Sheep Take A Hike
Written by Nancy Shaw and illustrated by Margot Apple (Houghton Mifflin Company, 1996)

"I Don't Care!" Said The Bear
Written and illustrated by Colin West (Candlewick Press, 1997)

Rhyming

Rhyming Skills Activities

Give Me A Sign

Remind students that rhyming words have the same ending sound, and provide several simple examples. Then read aloud a nursery rhyme or a poem. *Hand Rhymes*, collected and illustrated by Marc Brown (Puffin Books, 1993), and *Read-Aloud Rhymes For The Very Young*, selected by Jack Prelutsky and illustrated by Marc Brown (Alfred A. Knopf Books For Young Readers, 1986), are good poetry resources. Next say a pair of words from the rhyme or poem. Have students give the thumbs-up sign to indicate if the words rhyme and the thumbs-down sign if they don't. Continue with other selected word pairs in a similar fashion. What an easy way to actively engage all students and quickly check comprehension at the same time!

Recite-A-Rhyme

Recite a nursery rhyme or poem, empha-sizing the rhyming words. Ask students to join in with you and recite it several more times. After the children are familiar with the rhyme or poem, say it again. This time, however, each time you come to a rhyming word, instead of saying it, cup a hand by your ear and have students say the word in unison.

Bubble Gum Rhyme

Write the rhyme shown on chart paper and point to each word as you read it aloud to your class.

Ask students to identify the rhyming words in the poem. Read the poem again and direct students to clap whenever they hear words that rhyme. Have students brainstorm additional pairs of rhyming words. Illustrate children's ideas on construction-paper circles with simple pictures (one picture per circle and the corresponding picture rhyme on another circle of the same color). Mount the poem and the resulting gumballs on a bulletin board titled "Bubble Gum Rhymes." Add a gumball machine cutout to the display if desired.

Bubble gum, bubble gum, chew and blow.
Bubble gum, bubble gum, scrape your toe.
Bubble gum, bubble gum, tastes so sweet.
Get that bubble gum off your feet!

Rhyming

Rhyming Skills Activities

Box Of Rhymes

Try this activity for a hands-on review of rhyming words. Gather several objects with rhyming names. Place them in a large box that is decorated with brightly colored wrapping paper and labeled "Rhyme Box." Show students the objects in the box, one by one, and have students name them. Return the objects to the box. Next ask a student volunteer to close his eyes and take out two objects. He then opens his eyes and names the objects. The class gives the thumbs-up sign if the objects rhyme and the thumbs-down sign if they don't. The volunteer announces whether or not the words do indeed rhyme. Continue the activity until all students have taken a turn retrieving two objects from the box.

I Spy

This game is great when you have just a few minutes before a transition to another activity. Tell students that they are going to be detectives and solve rhyming mysteries. You will give them a clue, and they will need to identify the object in the room that you're describing. To play, think of an item in the room for which you can easily create a rhyme. Then announce, *"I spy something that rhymes with _____."* Have students share their guesses until someone correctly identifies your secret item. Continue the game in a similar fashion with different items. As students become more proficient with rhyming skills, have the student who correctly guesses the item give the next clue.

Suggested Objects For Rhyme Box

shell/bell	ring/string
toy car/star	book/hook
fork/cork	sock/clock
hat/toy cat	can/fan
bat/mat	shoe/glue

I spy something that rhymes with sock.

clock

Rhyming

Rhyming Skills Activities

Rhyming Shopping Spree

Develop students' auditory memory and rhyming skills with this game. When you prepare for this activity, you may want to refer to the list of common word endings (rimes) on page 92. Gather students in a circle on the floor and state, "I went shopping and I bought a…" Add an adjective with which students can easily rhyme a word. The student sitting to your left supplies a rhyming word to complete the sentence. Encourage students to repeat the sentence with you and then add another describing word to your shopping list. Have the next student in the circle provide a word that rhymes. Repeat the sentence with students including both pairs of rhyming words. Play continues around the circle until all students have taken a turn completing a rhyme.

I went shopping and I bought a red belt, a long song, and a wet pet.

Mix, Match, And Memory

To prepare this rhyming activity, make several pairs of rhyming picture cards with index cards and magazine pictures or simple illustrations. Place them in a pocket chart in random order. Ask a student volunteer to find two cards depicting objects that rhyme. Have the student place the cards together to make a pair. Have additional volunteers find and match the remaining rhymes.

Variations:
• Gather students in a circle on the floor and place the cards in the middle. Have students organize the scrambled cards into rhyming pairs.
• Place the cards in a learning center for individual students or small groups to match as described above or to use for a game of Rhyming Memory.

Rhyming Memory is played by turning all cards facedown in random order. The first player turns over two cards, states what they are, and announces if they rhyme. If the two cards rhyme, the player takes the cards and goes again. If they do not rhyme, he returns them to their original position and the next player takes a turn. Play continues until all of the matches have been found. The winner is the person who has the most matches.

Suggested Rhymes For "Mix, Match, And Memory"

sun/bun	house/mouse	man/fan
cat/hat	tree/bee	spoon/moon
mitten/kitten	pig/wig	dog/frog
bear/chair	book/hook	fish/dish

Alliteration

Alliteration is the repetition of initial sounds in two or more neighboring words—the perfect ingredient for tongue-tangling text. Youngsters' awareness of initial sounds is enhanced with exposure to alliteration, and children relish its playful nature. Share these entertaining books with students to teach them about alliteration in an engaging context.

Literature For Alliteration Lessons

Skill: Identify words that use alliteration
Context: Berenstains' B Book
Written and illustrated by Stan and Jan Berenstain (Random House Books For Young Readers, 1971)

This cumulative story uses alliteration to tell a zany tale that begins simply with a big brown bear. Students will undoubtedly delight in the comical illustrations and the tongue twister that builds throughout the book.

Tell students that most of the words in this story begin with the same special sound. Instruct students to listen for it carefully as you read the first few pages. Then have students identify the special sound—/b/. Finish reading the story, encouraging students to chime in with you. Afterward, revisit some of the pages and have students identify pictured objects that begin with /b/. For an added challenge, ask students to expand each word into a /b/ phrase, such as blowing bubbles or black bug's banana boxes.

black bug's banana boxes

Skill: Identify words that use alliteration
Context: Ridiculous Rhymes From A To Z
Written by John Walker and illustrated by David Catrow (Henry Holt And Company, Inc.; 1995)

Each letter of the alphabet is creatively represented in this lyrical book. Readers will meet fanciful characters such as a moose from Maine with mukluks, and Ida, who has insomnia and counts off iguanas instead of counting sheep. Your youngsters will undoubtedly erupt into gaggles of giggles when you share this comical story and accompanying illustrations.

After a first reading, revisit several of the pages and have students identify the alliterative words, using picture clues as necessary. The next day, tell students to listen extra carefully for words that begin with the same sound as you read the story again. Have students signal each time they hear alliteration by raising their hands. Stop after each set of pages and have students identify the alliterative words. Students will develop letter-perfect alliteration skills with this lesson!

Alliteration

Skill: Identify and produce words that use alliteration

Context: The A To Z Beastly Jamboree
Written and illustrated by Robert Bender (Dutton Children's Books, 1996)

An alliterative three-word sentence features a different animal interacting with its corresponding letter on each page of this book. Each page is uniquely bordered with all of the animals that have been introduced up to that point in the story. From ants anchoring Aa to zebras zippering Zz, this simple picture book will readily engage youngsters.

Read aloud the title and author. Before continuing with the text, show students each page of the book and encourage them to predict what the story is about. Read the story, pausing to have students say the letter names with you. Then create a class ABC book in several short sessions during the next few days.

To begin, write "Aa" in large letters on a sheet of drawing paper. Help students dictate a corresponding alliterative phrase. Write the dictated text on the page and assign a student to illustrate it. Continue in a like manner with the remaining letters of the alphabet. (Be sure to review the pages at the start of each session.) When all of the pages are completed, title another sheet of drawing paper "Our ABC Book." Laminate it for durability if desired. Compile and bind the sheets in alphabetical order with the cover. Read the published class book with students, and showcase it in your class library.

Literature For Developing Alliteration Skills

Berenstains' A Book
Written and illustrated by Stan and Jan Berenstain (Random House Books For Young Readers, 1997)

Six Sick Sheep: 101 Tongue Twisters
Written by Joanna Cole and Stephanie Calmenson and illustrated by Alan Tiegreen (William Morrow And Company, Inc.; 1993)

Alligator Arrived With Apples: A Potluck Alphabet Feast
Written by Crescent Dragonwagon and illustrated by Jose Aruego and Ariane Dewey (Simon & Schuster Children's Division, 1992)

The Awful Aardvarks Go To School
Written by Reeve Lindbergh and illustrated by Tracey Campbell Pearson (Viking Penguin, 1997)

Alison's Zinnia
Written and illustrated by Anita Lobel (William Morrow And Company, Inc.; 1996)

A My Name Is…
Written by Alice Lyne and illustrated by Lynne Cravath (Whispering Coyote Press, Inc.; 1997)

Alligators All Around: An Alphabet
by Maurice Sendak (HarperCollins Children's Books, 1991)

Alliteration

Alliteration Skills Activities

Nifty New Names

Teach students to recite "Wee Willie Winkie" (found below). Then help each student transform his own name into a two- or three-word alliterative phrase. For example, "Sue" might become "Super Silly Sue," and "Ted" might change to "Terrific Ted." Take turns substituting each child's alliterative name for "Wee Willie Winkie" and recite the resulting rhyme. Students will certainly enjoy this personalized approach to alliteration!

Wee Willie Winkie

Wee Willie Winkie runs through the town,
Upstairs and downstairs in his nightgown.
Rapping at the window, crying through the lock,
"Are the children all in bed, for now it's eight o'clock!"

What's My Rule?

In advance, compose several alliterative sentences or use the list below. Tell students to listen carefully to the sentence that you're about to say. Explain that all of the words in the sentence follow a special rule and that youngsters need to identify the rule. Then say an alliterative sentence such as, *"Cats can catch caterpillars,"* emphasizing the beginning phoneme of each word. Have students repeat the sentence together, then identify the rule. *(All of the words begin with /c/.)* Continue the activity with other alliterative sentences.

Sample Alliterative Sentences

Boys bounce balls.
School starts soon.
Go get gooey gum.
People pick pink packages.
Fantastic fish find fabulous fun.
Max mows Mary's meadow.
Nine nifty nurses need new notebooks.
Dotted dalmatians dance daily.
Hungry hippos hope Hal has hamburgers.
Rita received really red roses.

Super Silly Sue

Lovely Lucy

Fun, Fabulous Franklin

Alliteration

Alliteration Skills Activities

Simply School Supplies

Look for alliteration right in your own classroom! Walk around the classroom pointing out a variety of items, one at a time. Have students suggest a descriptive word that starts with the same sound as each item; then direct the class to repeat the resulting phrase. Students might give school objects new names such as *terrific toys, wide windows, rough rug, and fun fingerpaints.*

Fun Fingerpaints

My Name Is…

Try this variation of a traditional rhyme to reinforce alliteration skills. Gather students in a circle on the floor. Model a simple clapping pattern such as *pat, clap, pat, clap.* Have students practice with you until they are able to maintain the rhythm. Then add words. Start by saying, *"A, my name is Alice, and I sell apples"* while you continue the clapping pattern. Continue with each letter of the alphabet in a similar manner by saying the letter and name phrase, and then having the next student in the circle supply the ending phrase.

Tongue Twister Time

Read aloud several tongue twisters—*Six Sick Sheep: 101 Tongue Twisters* written by Joanna Cole and Stephanie Calmenson and illustrated by Alan Tiegreen (William Morrow And Company, Inc.; 1993) is a great source. Recite a selected tongue twister several times as quickly as possible; then have student volunteers do the same. Next write some original tongue twisters with students, and record them on chart paper. Invite the principal or another school staff member for a Tongue Twister Challenge. Have student volunteers try their hand at saying one of the student-created tongue twisters several times quickly. Then challenge your guest to say some tongue twisters. After students and your guest attempt several different tongue twisters, offer them a tasty treat, such as luscious lollipops or appetizing apples, to top off the day.

Oddity Skills Activities

Oddity tasks involve comparing and contrasting specific sounds. For example, learners may be presented with three words orally and asked to identify the word that begins with a different sound than the other two. Learners may also be asked to determine similarities and differences based on rhymes or on middle or final sounds.

Oddity tasks are appropriate for kindergartners, particularly if pictures or other visual cues are provided. As students' proficiency increases, such cues are no longer necessary. Oddity activities progress in difficulty from those involving rhymes, to those focusing on beginning and ending sounds, to those featuring vowel or medial sounds. Literature used to target rhyming and alliteration skills lends itself to oddity skills lessons, too.

Which One Rhymes?

Use the Alphapix on pages 78–84 for individual or small-group practice with oddity skills. Show students three Alphapix. Say two words that rhyme with one of the picture cards. Have students indicate which picture rhymes with the two words. Continue with other pictures and pairs of rhyming words. Increase the number of picture cards shown at one time as students' skills improve.

Thumbs-Up!

Give thumbs-up to rhymes. Explain to students that you will say sets of words. Students will signal with the thumbs-up sign if the words rhyme and thumbs-down if they don't. Say the following chant to introduce each set of words:

Listen carefully to me this time.
Show thumbs-up if these words rhyme!

Then say two or three words and ask students to signal if the words rhyme or not. Repeat with different sets of words. Students' proficiency can be determined at a glance with this hands-on lesson!

Which one rhymes with wish and dish?

Oddity Skills Activities

Which One Doesn't Belong?

Tell students that they will need to listen carefully to the final sounds of words. Explain that one word in each group does not belong because it ends with a different sound. Say three words, two of which end with the same phoneme and one that does not, such as "cat," "toy," and "sat." Have students tell you which word does not belong. Continue with different sets of words.

Variations:

* Provide visual clues with picture cards or objects.
* Select three students—two with names that end with the same phoneme. Ask all three students to stand. Challenge their classmates to determine which student's name ends with a different sound. Then select three different students and continue in a similar fashion.

Which word doesn't belong?

Rule Breakers

This beginning-sound oddity task builds on the skills learned in "What's My Rule?" (page 36). Modify an alliterative sentence to include one word that does not follow the beginning-sound rule. For example, you could change "Boys bounce balls" to "Boys bounce red balls." Say the new sentence and have students identify the rule-breaking word—"red." Repeat the activity in a similar manner with other sentences.

Look And Listen

Help students tune in to beginning sounds. Show students three objects. Tell students that only two of the items begin with the same sound. Youngsters need to determine which object begins with a different sound. Say the names of the objects. Then have students repeat the words with you. Ask students to identify the object that starts with a different phoneme. Repeat with additional sets of objects.

truck   train   ball

Color Cues

Different colors of construction paper are all you need for this ending-sound activity. Show students a sheet of red construction paper. Tell them to listen for the ending sound when you say the corresponding color word. Next say two other words, only one of which ends with /d/, such as "bed" and "sun." Ask students to determine which word ends with the same sound as "red." After they identify the correct word, continue the activity with other colors of paper and pairs of words.

red

Blending

Blending tasks require learners to combine phonemes to produce words. Some of the different ways to teach blending are outlined here. The tasks listed progress from those that are usually the easiest to those that are typically the most challenging.

Present the learner with

- two words that combine to make a compound word
  Example: birth day

- syllables
  Example: pa per

- two word parts—The first part ends with the vowel, and the second part is everything after the vowel.
  Example: ba t

- two word parts—The first part is everything before the vowel, and the second part includes the vowel and everything after it.
  Example: b at

- isolated phonemes
  Example: /b/ /a/ /t/

Literature For Blending Lessons

Skill: Blend words to form compound words
Context: The Snowy Day
by Ezra Jack Keats (Puffin Books, 1976)

Collages and simple text describe Peter's adventures in newly fallen snow. He happily creates different footprints and tracks, makes a snowman and snow angels, and slides on a mountain of snow. He's later disappointed, however, when he discovers that his attempt to keep a snowball in his coat pocket was unsuccessful. Another snowstorm the next day quickly transforms Peter's sadness to joy, and he's ready for more fun in the snow.

Share this entertaining picture book with your youngsters. Then tell students that you noticed these special words in the story: snowsuit, snowman, and snowball. Ask students to guess why these words are special. *(Each of the words begins with "snow.")* Explain that you are going to break apart these special words, and students will put them back together. Say each compound word again, this time breaking down the word into two words. Direct students to blend the word *snow* with other words.

Use the following list of snow-related compound words in a similar manner for more practice with blending.

Suggested Compound Words

snowbank	snowbird
snowfall	snowflake
snowblower	snowdrift
snowmobile	snowplow
snowstorm	

Blending

Skill: Blend the final phoneme with the rest of the word
Context: Hattie And The Fox
Written by Mem Fox and illustrated by Patricia Mullins (Simon & Schuster Children's Division, 1992)

Hattie is startled to see a nose peeking through the bushes one day. Her barnyard friends react to this news with indifference followed by concern as more of the mysterious figure is revealed. Children are sure to chime in with the animals' lively conversation as the story progresses.

After reading aloud this predictable story, have students name each of the animals in the book. Record the list on chart paper and draw a simple picture clue beside each word. Then say each word, breaking it down into two parts—ending the first part with the vowel and including the remaining letters in the second part (pi g, for example). Ask students to blend the sounds and say the words. Invite students to brainstorm other farm animals. Add these animal names to the list and use them for extra blending practice.

Skill: Blend isolated phonemes
Context: Green Eggs And Ham
by Dr. Seuss (Random House Books For Young Readers, 1966)

Here or there, this cumulative tale is guaranteed to delight youngsters. Sam persistently and creatively attempts to entice the main character to taste green eggs and ham. After a series of comical adventures that take the characters in a car, on a train, and on a boat, the main character finally relents. He reluctantly tastes the green eggs and ham and is pleased to discover that he does indeed like these unusual foods.

After reading this humorous book to students, tell them that you've chosen some mystery words from the story. Students will need to be sound detectives to determine the words. Give the sounds of each word in isolation—/s/ /a/ /m/, for example. Have students solve the mysteries by blending each set of sounds into a word.

Suggested Mystery Words			
Sam	ham	train	rain
house	mouse	goat	boat
tree	see		

Literature For Developing Blending Skills

There Was An Old Lady Who Swallowed A Fly
Illustrated by Pam Adams (Child's Play [International] Ltd, 1989)

Elephants Aloft
Written by Kathi Appelt and illustrated by Keith Baker (Harcourt Brace & Company, 1995)

The Wind Blew
Written and illustrated by Pat Hutchins (Simon & Schuster Children's Division, 1993)

Rain
Written by Robert Kalan and illustrated by Donald Crews (William Morrow And Company, 1991)

Blending

Word Recipes

Blend may be a new vocabulary word for many youngsters. Define it by comparing the process of sound blending to cooking. Explain to students that a recipe uses separate ingredients. People put ingredients together in a special way to make something to eat. Similarly, individual sounds are the ingredients for words. We combine the sounds in a particular order to make words.

Bring this analogy to life with an appetizing project. Use a blender or an electric mixer to make eggnog, milkshakes, or instant pudding with students.

Hear, Say, And Do

This activity engages students in listening, blending phonemes, and movement. Separate an action word into isolated sounds. Direct students to blend the sounds together to make the word. Then have students perform the corresponding action.

Suggested Action Words

sit
hop
tap
wink
wave
stand
blink
clap
jump
skip

March And Jump

Prepare a word list in advance. You may choose words from literature that you've shared recently, a thematic unit, or other curricular areas. Have students stand in front of you. Say a sentence with one of the words, emphasizing the chosen word. Then say the selected word as a series of sounds. March in place as you do so, taking one step for each phoneme. Then have students blend the phonemes and say the word, jumping once in place. For example, say, *"I have a black and white cat."* Then say, *"/k/ /a/ /t/,"* taking one step for each sound. Next have students blend these phonemes and say "cat" as they jump once in place.

Variation: Snap And Clap

Complete this activity in a similar manner. Instead of marching, however, snap your fingers with each phoneme. Have students clap as they blend the sounds.

Blending

Say It Fast!

This sound-blending activity takes just a few minutes. Say each phoneme of a word. Instruct students to say the sounds fast to make the word. You may choose to use classroom words and students' names for added interest.

To vary the activity, introduce each series of sounds with one of the following rhymes:

Remember the sounds that you heard.
Blend them now to make a word.

Blend all the sounds that you hear.
Say the word loud and clear.

Listen to me say it slow.
Now say it fast. Here we go!

Listen, listen with your ears.
Say the word that you hear.

Colorful Blends

Cut a six-inch square from each of the eight basic colors of construction paper: red, yellow, blue, green, orange, purple, brown, and black. Display the squares on your chalkboard ledge or in a pocket chart. Say a color word. Next direct students to say and clap each syllable of the word. Then ask a student volunteer to identify the matching paper square and put it on his desktop. Repeat with the remaining colors. After all of the squares have been taken, tell students that they are going to put away the squares in a special way. Say a color word as before, but this time isolate each of the phonemes. Have a student tell the class the word, retrieve the corresponding color square from his classmate's desk, and return the square to its original place.

Segmenting

Segmenting refers to the process of breaking apart words into phonemes. Segmenting and blending tasks are similar because they both involve separating words in some manner. With blending tasks, teachers isolate the phonemes. With segmenting tasks, however, students separate the sounds. Some of the different types of segmenting tasks are described below.

The learner isolates

- syllables
  Example: pa per

- the initial sound
  Example: "Bat" begins with /b/.

- the final sound
  Example: "Bat" ends with /t/.

- the middle sound
  Example: The middle sound in "bat" is /a/.

- each sound (This task often involves counting or tapping sounds.)
  Example: /b/ /a/ /t/

Literature For Segmenting Lessons

Skill: Isolate and count syllables
Context: From Head To Toe
Written and illustrated by Eric Carle
(HarperCollins Children's Books, 1997)

This interactive book invites youngsters to imitate several animals' antics. Children will develop an "I can do it" attitude as they clap, wriggle, and bend like the animals depicted in Eric Carle's collages.

Encourage children to try the movements described in the story as you read it aloud. Then tell students that they will determine which animal words have just one part, which have two, and which have three. Have students generate a list of the animals in the book. Use simple picture clues to list the animals on chart paper. Then say the first animal word. Have the children repeat the word with you, clapping as you say each syllable. Record the number of claps beside the picture of the animal. Continue in a like manner with the rest of the words. Help students summarize the information shown on the chart.

Variation: Make a picture card to correspond with each animal word. Say, clap, and count the word parts for the first animal with students. Have a student volunteer make a Unifix® cube tower with the corresponding number of cubes. Place the picture card beside the tower. Repeat these steps with the remaining animal words. Assist students in rearranging the cards and towers to group animal words with the same number of parts. They'll be able to see at a glance which words have one, two, or three parts. Not only will students' ability to segment words improve, but their counting skills and number concepts will be reinforced as well.

Segmenting

Skill: Isolate initial sounds
Context: Ten Black Dots
Written and illustrated by Donald Crews
(William Morrow And Company, Inc.; 1995)

What can you do with ten black dots? This simple picture book provides plenty of suggestions. From using one dot to make a sun, to using ten dots to create balloons in a tree, readers will find imaginative ideas throughout this book.

After sharing this delightful book with students, revisit several pages. Ask students to name the objects shown. Then have students isolate the initial sound of each object named. Next invite students to brainstorm other objects that can be made with black dots. Have each student use crayons, glue, and ten or fewer black circle cutouts to create a picture on a sheet of drawing paper. After all students have completed their work, ask each child to share her picture with the class. Have her identify the initial sound of the illustrated object as well. Collect the pictures and display them on a brightly colored bulletin board titled "Lots Of Dots."

Skill: Isolate final sounds
Context: Shoes From Grandpa
Written by Mem Fox and illustrated by Patricia Mullins (Orchard Books, 1992)

Grandpa notices that Jessie has outgrown her clothes, so he buys a new pair of shoes for her. His action prompts other family members to go shopping, too. They each buy clothing to go with Jessie's new shoes. But Jessie wants something much more practical than the pretty clothes that she receives.

Read aloud this cumulative tale, inviting students to chime in with you. Then have students name an article of clothing that Jessie received. Repeat the word, emphasizing the final phoneme. Ask students to isolate the ending sound. Continue the activity by having students recall the other articles of clothing in the story and isolate the final sound of each word. For an added challenge, ask students to determine which words end with the same sound.

More Literature For Segmenting Lessons

This Is The House That Jack Built
Written and illustrated by Pam Adams
(Child's Play [International] Ltd, 1977)

Count!
Written and illustrated by Denise Fleming
(Henry Holt And Company, Inc.; 1997)

Little Blue And Little Yellow
Written and illustrated by Leo Lionni (William Morrow And Company, Inc.; 1995)

Whose Hat?
Written and illustrated by Margaret Miller
(Greenwillow Books, 1988)

Cookie's Week
Written by Cindy Ward and illustrated by Tomie dePaola (The Putnam Publishing Group, 1997)

One Day In The Jungle
Written and illustrated by Colin West
(Candlewick Press, 1997)

Segmenting

Counting Sounds

Here are some strategies students can use to count phonemes.
For every sound, instruct each student to

- clap his hands
- tap his desktop with a fingertip or pencil
- make a check mark or dot on paper
- march in place
- place a counter on his desk

For extra blending practice, count the phonemes. Then have students blend the sounds and say the word.

Segmenting Rhymes

Use these rhymes to introduce words for segmenting exercises:

Listen, listen to the word.
How many sounds can be heard?

Listen now with your ears.
Count the sounds that you hear.

Words are short, words are long.
Hear the sounds and clap along.

Listen, listen to the word.
Say the first sound that you heard.

Listen now with your ears.
Say the last sound that you hear.

Segmenting

Name Game

To reinforce initial sounds, ask a student volunteer to stand in front of the class. Have him announce his name. Repeat his name, emphasizing the initial sound. Direct students to say that sound in isolation. Next have students raise their hands if their own names begin with the same phoneme. One at a time, ask each of these students to say his name and come to the front of the class. Then choose another volunteer. Have students identify the initial phoneme of the new volunteer's name. Continue the game as before until everyone is standing at the front of the room.

Then tell students that they will return to their seats in a special way. Say a sound and have students whose names begin with that sound return to their seats. Vary the game by focusing on the last sound of students' names rather than the first.

Animal Names

Say the name of an animal. Ask students to repeat the word with you. Have a student isolate the initial sound. Then lead students in this chant:

[Child's name], s/he just knew.
Everyone, let's say it, too!

Then have students repeat the initial sound in isolation three times and say the word (/b/ /b/ /b/ bear, for example). Repeat with other animal words.

Variation: Stand animal picture cards on your chalkboard ledge with the pictures turned toward the chalkboard. Ask a student volunteer to select a card and turn it to show the picture. The class says the name of the animal, and the activity continues as described above.

How Many Parts?

Prepare a graph on a large sheet of paper in advance. Program the horizontal axis, as shown, for the number of parts (syllables) in children's names. Program the vertical axis for a number of students. Have each student determine how many parts are in her first name. Clapping or tapping syllables may facilitate this step. One at a time, instruct each student to color a section of the graph to show how many parts her name has. After everyone has had a turn, help students analyze and summarize the information shown on the graph. For an interesting extension, graph last names in a similar manner and compare the two graphs.

How Many Parts Does Your Name Have?

Phonemic Manipulation

Manipulation tasks are some of the most challenging phonemic activities. Some advanced kindergartners may be ready for these complex tasks. To successfully complete such a task, learners must be able to isolate as well as blend phonemes. Students must also be able to remember phonemic information from one step of the task to the next. Phonemic manipulation tasks involve adding, deleting, or moving phonemes to make new words or nonwords. Here are some examples of manipulation exercises.

The teacher provides these instructions:

- Say "birdhouse." Say it again but don't say "bird."
- Say "birdhouse." Say it again but don't say "house."
- Say "birdhouse." Say it again but instead of "bird" say "dog."

- Say "bat" without /b/.
- Say "bat" without /t/.
- Say "bat." Say it again but instead of /b/ say /m/.

Phonemic Manipulation Activities

Take-Away Sounds

Try this manipulation task with advanced students. Create a word list. (Words with common endings are good choices for kindergartners.) Say one of the words. Ask students to take away its beginning sound and say the remaining phonemes.

Missing Sounds

Tell students that you are going to change one of their names by taking away a sound. Students will need to put the name back together with the missing sound. Say a student's name, omitting the initial sound. The student whose name was said stands. He and his classmates say his name, including the first sound. The student sits down, and play continues until all students' names have been called.

Phonemic Manipulation

Phoneme Mix-Ups

Tell students that the class is going to play a *"fame."* Students are bound to respond, "A what?" Explain that you meant to say "game." Compliment students for being such sharp listeners and noticing your error. Tell students that their good listening skills will come in handy with this activity.

Say a sentence with one word that has an incorrect beginning phoneme. Have students identify the mixed-up word and replace the wrong sound with the correct one.

Sample Sentences
Open the **floor**. (door)
Put on your **boat**. (coat)
I am **hive** years old. (five)
I want to read a **look**. (book)
I have new **blues**. (shoes)
Apples are **bed**. (red)
Grass is **mean**. (green)

Literature Connection

Skill: Manipulate phonemes
Context: Don't Forget The Bacon!
Written and illustrated by Pat Hutchins
(William Morrow And Company, Inc.; 1989)

This humorous book is a wonderful example of how changing a few phonemes significantly alters meaning. A mother orally provides her son with her shopping list and sends him to the grocery store. As he mentally rehearses the list, he inadvertently changes phonemes of several words, resulting in an extremely different list.

After reading aloud this entertaining story, return to the page with the original shopping list and reread it. Invite students to recall how the list changed as the story progressed. Ask students to identify the specific sound substitutions that the boy made.

For added fun, use props to retell the story. Students will delight in seeing firsthand how the boy's confusion results in such a ridiculous list.

Phonics

Phonics refers to the relationship between oral and written language. Phonics skills are strongest when they are built on a foundation of phonemic awareness. Children with an understanding of letter-sound relationships combined with strong phonemic awareness develop better word-recognition and spelling skills.

You can build youngsters' visual familiarity with letters, letter-identification skills, and letter-sound knowledge in the context of meaningful reading and writing experiences. Your students will also benefit from hands-on phonics lessons.

Literature For Phonics Lessons

Use these engaging alphabet books for a variety of letter-sound lessons.

Skill: Letter identification
Context: Arlene Alda's ABC
Written and photographed by Arlene Alda (Tricycle Press, 1993)

The photos in this unique book cleverly reinforce students' visual perceptions of letters. Readers discover that many common objects form letters or have letters hidden within them.

Show students the cover of the book and read the title. Explain that this ABC book is special because it shows that many ordinary objects form letters or have letters hidden within them. Direct students' attention to the photograph of the apple. Trace the edge of the apple with your finger to show youngsters that it forms a *B*. Share the book with students, encouraging them to identify the object shown on each page. Trace the hidden letter in each photo and have children name the letter.

Then challenge students to find hidden letters in classroom objects. Each time a student discovers such a letter, hold a letter card beside the item to make a comparison (reproducible on pages 12–17). Review the book the next day. Then take students on a walk to find more hidden letters.

Skill: Letter identification
Context: Chicka Chicka Boom Boom
Written by Bill Martin, Jr., and John Archambault and illustrated by Lois Ehlert (Simon & Schuster Books For Young Readers, 1989)

Each letter of the alphabet races to the top of a coconut tree in this charming story. Unfortunately, the tree bends greatly under the weight of the letters, and they all topple to the ground. Tangled, knotted, and twisted, the letters dust themselves off and ready themselves for another race to the top of the tree.

After a first reading, have students pat their legs or snap their fingers in unison as you reread the story. Then revisit the illustrations and ask students to identify letters that you describe. For example, ask youngsters to tell you which letter has a Band-Aid® and which letters are orange.

Next help students create an alphabet tree for your class bulletin board. To begin, cut out a brown trunk, green leaves, and several brown coconuts from bulletin-board paper. Assemble the pieces to make a coconut tree. Assign each letter of the alphabet to a student. Have each youngster use a stencil to trace a letter on brightly colored construction paper; then cut out his letter. Assist the children in mounting the letters on and around the tree. Use the display for quick letter review. Point to letters and ask students to name them, or describe a letter and have students guess its identity.

Variation:

Distribute cut-out letters to students. Have students decorate the letters with crayons, colorful paper scraps, and Band-Aids®. Reread the story. After each page, ask the students whose letters were just named to identify them and then add the letters to the display.

Skills: Letter identification and letter-sound associations
Context: It Begins With An A
Written by Stephanie Calmenson and illustrated by Marisabina Russo (Hyperion Books For Children, 1994)

This alphabet riddle book will put students' thinking skills to the test. Each page of this interactive book has a riddle with four rhyming clues. Each beginning letter is clearly featured in the illustrations. A picture-coded answer key is provided for young readers to practice reading independently.

Challenge students to guess the answer to each riddle as you read this book aloud. Then have students create their own ABC riddles. To begin, write each letter of the alphabet on chart paper. Have students brainstorm a word for each letter. Record children's responses with words and simple picture clues. Then have each student select a letter and item from the list. Instruct him to write the letter on a sheet of white construction paper and draw the item. As students work, have each youngster dictate a clue about his chosen object for you to record on his paper. When students have completed their work, invite each child to share his riddle and have his classmates guess the answer. Then direct the youngster to show his illustration to reveal the answer.

Skill: Letter-sound associations
Context: F-Freezing ABC
Written and illustrated by Posy Simmonds (Alfred A. Knopf Books For Young Readers, 1996)

The shivering animals in this frosty book are a-absolutely f-f-freezing. Their desperate search for warm lodging takes them on an alphabet adventure from the elephants' cramped quarters to a wave-battered lighthouse. When at last they return to their home, they discover that Elephant has thoughtfully warmed it for them. The only problem is that it's a bit too warm now!

Take advantage of the wintry context of this story to build letter-sound associations. As you read each shivery word, pause after the initial sound. Invite students to finish the word. Then engage students in a discussion about how the animals treated each other. Faced with the cold weather, the animals neglected their manners. Revisit several pages and have students role-play a more polite version.

Skills: Letter identification and sound association
Context: Eating The Alphabet: Fruits & Vegetables From A To Z
Written and illustrated by Lois Ehlert (Harcourt Brace & Company, 1996)

Serve up an appetizing look at the alphabet with this collection of brightly colored illustrations. Each page of this book features a letter and several examples of fruits and vegetables that begin with it. Two labels are shown for each food—one in uppercase letters and the other in lowercase letters. A glossary packed with information about each fruit and vegetable provides lots of fun facts to share.

Introduce students to common and less-familiar fruits and vegetables in alphabetical order with this book. Have students identify the letter and the foods shown on each page. Take this opportunity to tell students about each of the foods.

Follow up this session by making a class fruit and vegetable book. Using Ehlert's work as a model, have each child make a watercolor illustration of her favorite fruit or vegetable. Help her label the picture with the name of the food and the beginning letter. Bind the pages with a cover in ABC order.

Celebrate a job well done with a healthful snack of fruits and vegetables, such as apples, cucumbers, and oranges. Provide each student with a sample of a variety of fruits and vegetables to enjoy as you share the completed class book.

Skills: Letter identification and sound/picture associations

Context: Have You Ever Seen…? Written and illustrated by Beau Gardner (BGA Publishing, Inc.; 1994)

Have you ever seen a banana with buttons or a turtle with a tie? If not, be sure to check out this creative ABC book. Youngsters will undoubtedly erupt into loads of laughter as you share each unique animal and object.

After an initial read-through, return to the first page. Reread the page; then ask students to identify the letter and the alliterative words. Continue with the remaining pages in a like manner. Then have each student create his own alliterative animal or object on brightly colored construction paper. Help him label the picture and have him write the corresponding letter at the top of his paper. Mount the completed pictures on a bulletin board titled "Have You Ever Seen…?"

Pink popcorn parrot playing Ping-Pong®?

Pink popcorn parrot playing Ping-Pong®?

Literature For Letter Skills Lessons

Old Black Fly
Written by Jim Aylesworth and illustrated by Stephen Gammell (Henry Holt And Company, Inc.; 1995)

Clifford's ABC
Written and illustrated by Norman Bridwell (Scholastic Inc., 1994)

The ABC Mystery
Written and illustrated by Doug Cushman (HarperCollins Children's Books, 1996)

Ape In A Cape
Written and illustrated by Fritz Eichenberg (Harcourt Brace & Company, 1988)

The Letters Are Lost!
Written and illustrated by Lisa Campbell Ernst (Viking Children's Books, 1996)

C Is For City
Written by Nikki Grimes and illustrated by Pat Cummings (Lothrop, Lee & Shepard Books; 1995)

Crazy ABC
Written by Judy Hindley and illustrated by Nick Sharratt (Candlewick Press, 1996)

26 Letters And 99 Cents
Written and illustrated by Tana Hoban (William Morrow And Company, Inc.; 1995)

Alphabet Book
Written by Lara Tankel Holtz and photographed by Dave King (Dorling Kindersley Publishing, Inc.; 1997)

David McPhail's Animals A To Z
Written and illustrated by David McPhail (Scholastic Inc., 1989)

Hands-On Phonics Materials And Activities

These hands-on materials and alphabet activities build students' letter skills. Introduce each material and activity in a whole-group lesson. After demonstrating how to use and put away these new materials and activities, store the supplies in a classroom Alphabet Activity Center. Provide opportunities for students to explore the materials in the center independently or with partners.

Alpha-Sock Game

Put socks without mates to good use with this letter-recognition activity. Place several magnetic or foam letters in a sock. Have a student reach into the sock and grab a letter. Ask him to guess what letter it is without taking it out of the sock. Then direct him to pull the letter out of the sock. If he guessed correctly, he may keep the letter. If his guess was incorrect, have him return the letter to the sock. Continue the activity until students have successfully identified all of the letters.

Sorting Letters

Write each letter of the alphabet on a separate small paper bag. Open the bags and stand them up on the floor. Then arrange the bags in alphabetical order. Give each student a magnetic or foam letter, letter tile, or letter card. Have each student, in turn, name his letter and drop it into the corresponding bag.

Variations:
- When a student drops the letter into the bag, ask him to describe the letter's relative position in the alphabet. For example, a student who identifies *B* might state that *B* comes after *A* and before *C*.
- After all of the letters have been sorted, lead the class in an ABC song, pointing to each letter bag as you sing. Then have students close their eyes while you remove a letter bag. Ask students to open their eyes and guess which letter is missing. As students' proficiency increases, remove more bags at one time.
- Have students help you arrange the bags in ABC order prior to the sorting activity. Start by having students order only the first several letters of the alphabet. Increase the number of letters as students' skills improve.
- Conclude the activity by naming letters at random and directing students to pick up and put away the corresponding bags.

Hands-On Phonics Materials And Activities

Disappearing Letters

Place three or four magnetic letters on a small magnetic surface such as a burner cover or cookie tray. Review each of the letter names with students. Then turn the surface from students' view and remove one of the letters. Show the children the remaining letters and say this chant:

Take a look. It's time to see.
The missing letter—
What could it be?

After students correctly guess which letter you took, put it back on the magnetic surface. Review the letter names again and continue the activity. As students' visual memory and letter-identification skills improve, increase the number of letters presented and taken away at one time.

Order And Pair

Create letter manipulatives for this center activity with plastic counters or poker chips. Use a permanent marker to write each upper- and lowercase letter on a separate counter or chip. Make a dot below each letter to help students correctly orient the letters. Store uppercase letters in one container and lowercase letters in another. Depending on your students' ability, you may want to present only half of the upper- and lowercase letters initially. Display an alphabet strip above the letter containers.

Have each student arrange the uppercase letters in ABC order, referring to the alphabet strip as necessary. Ask him to place the lowercase letters below the corresponding uppercase letters.

Tactile Letters

Tap into students' sense of touch by making these fun-to-feel letters. Provide time for students to explore these letters at your Alphabet Activity Center. Then use them for letter-recognition and letter-matching lessons.

Sandpaper Letters
Draw letters on sandpaper. Cut out the letters and paste them onto tagboard cards. Glue a sandpaper dot below each letter to distinguish top from bottom if desired.

Glittery Glue Letters
Print each letter of the alphabet on a separate tagboard card. Trace each letter with glitter glue and let it dry. Add another coat of glue and a dot of glue below the letter if desired.

Letter Potpourri
After writing each letter of the alphabet on a separate tagboard card, outline the letter with a thick line of glue. Press dried beans, unpopped popcorn, or lengths of yarn into the glue. Glue a bean, kernel of popcorn, or snippet of yarn below each letter to provide an orientation clue for students. Let the glue dry overnight. Then add another line of glue.

Hands-On Phonics Materials And Activities

Stamparama

Provide ABC rubber stamps at your Alphabet Activity Center. Look for sets of upper- and lowercase letter stamps at your local teacher supply store. Give children play experiences with these letter stamps before using the stamps for teacher-directed activities.

Stamp-A-Name

In advance, write each student's name on a separate sentence strip. Have each student refer to his sentence strip as he uses stamps to spell his name. For an added challenge, ask each child to stamp his last name, too. Be sure to remind him to leave space between his first and last name.

Animal "Stamp-ede"

Duplicate a class supply of papers with this sentence starter: "See the _____." Have each child draw her favorite animal on her paper. As the students work, ask each one to identify her animal. Lightly write the animal word on the blank, leaving extra space between each letter. After students complete their illustrations, direct youngsters to stamp each letter of the animal name on your corresponding handwritten letters. Display the students' completed work on a brightly colored bulletin board titled "Our Animal 'Stamp-ede.' "

Stamp Around

Use letter stamps and discarded magazines to create a one-of-a-kind ABC book. To begin, assign each letter of the alphabet to a student. Have each child create a border on a large sheet of white drawing paper with the corresponding letter stamp. Then instruct him to cut out magazine pictures of objects that begin with that letter. Have him paste the pictures inside the letter border. Write the title "Stamp Around The ABCs" on a sheet of paper and decorate it as desired to create a cover. Compile the pages in alphabetical order and bind them with the cover to make a unique addition to your classroom library.

Calendar Cutouts

Precut calendar pieces come in a variety of colors and seasonal shapes. Purchase cutouts that complement the units or concepts that you are teaching. To make calendar cutout cards for phonics lessons, glue the cutouts onto sentence strips, leaving space between each shape. Use a permanent marker to print either an upper- or lowercase letter beside each cutout. Cut the strips into individual letter cards as shown and laminate them. (Glue any extra cutouts onto sentence strips. Cut them into cards and laminate them as well. If a letter is lost, use a permanent marker to write the missing letter on an extra card to create a replacement card in a jiffy.)

These versatile calendar cutout cards are perfect for a wide range of letter skills activities. For example, ask students to sequence them in alphabetical order or pair upper- and lowercase letters.

Hands-On Phonics Materials And Activities

ABC Manipulatives

Transform your alphabet bulletin-board set or strip into letter manipulatives. To do so, cut the set or strip apart into individual letter cards and laminate them. Use these clever cut-ups for the letter skills activities described below.

Runaway Letters

Place the letter cards on the chalkboard ledge in ABC order. Ask students to close their eyes while you remove one letter. Have students open their eyes and guess what letter is missing. After the youngsters correctly identify the letter, return it to the ledge. Repeat the activity with different letters in a similar manner. As students' skills progress, remove a greater number of cards at one time.

Puzzling Letters

This self-checking task is perfect for an independent or center activity. Cut apart each letter and its corresponding picture into two puzzle-shaped pieces as shown. Have students match the letters with the pictures to complete the puzzles.

Alphabet Lineup

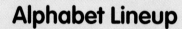

Distribute the letter cards to students. Call out "A." Have the student who has this letter place it on the chalkboard ledge. Call out "B" and direct the student who has that card to place it beside A. Continue this activity until the entire alphabet is lined up on the ledge.

To extend the activity, tell students to guess the letters that you describe. Provide clues such as "I am thinking of the letter that is between A and C." Use key words such as before, between, and after to reinforce preposition concepts as well as letter-identification skills.

Clip A Letter

Hang a clothesline at students' level to prepare this sequencing activity. (Be sure to check with your school's custodian before securing the clothesline to the wall.) Have children use clothespins to clip the alphabet cards to the clothesline in ABC order. Store the alphabet cards and clothespins in a small laundry basket when not in use.

Alphabet Stepping Stones

For this letter-identification game, children try to cross your classroom river while avoiding the alligators lurking about the alphabet stepping stones. Prepare the game by cutting 26 stones from gray or brown paper. Write each letter of the alphabet on a separate stone. Enlarge, duplicate, and cut out the pattern below to create paper alligators. Spread out the stones on the floor and place the alligators in the river among the stones as shown. Challenge students to cross the river by stepping on the stones without touching the alligators. Ask each student to name each letter as he steps on the corresponding stone. Continue until all students have taken a turn.

Pattern For "Alphabet Stepping Stones"

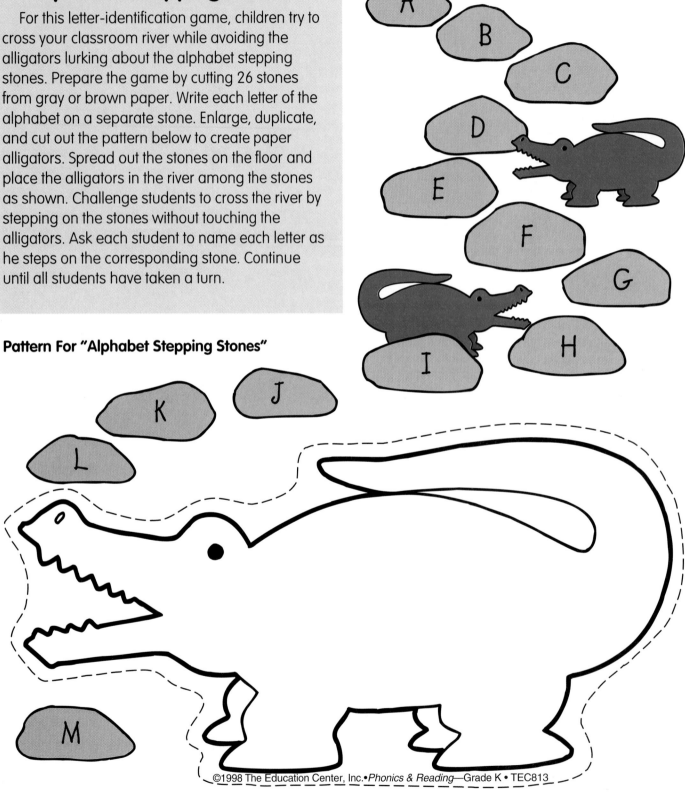

©1998 The Education Center, Inc.•*Phonics & Reading*—Grade K • TEC813

Build-A-Word Card Activities

Directions and reproducible patterns for making Build-A-Word cards are found on pages 11–17. You may also want to check your local teacher supply store for preprinted Build-A-Word Cards from your friends at The Mailbox®.

Sing And Step

Have students stand in a circle. Give each student a large alphabet card. If you have more than 26 students, use extra letters to ensure that everyone will be actively involved. Slowly sing an alphabet song with students. As you sing, have each child take one step into the circle when the letter that she is holding is named. Then repeat the song, but this time have students take a step back when they hear their letters. Ask students to trade letter cards with classmates and complete the activity once more.

Show Me!

Choose five letters to practice with this fast-paced letter-recognition activity. Give each child a student set of the selected letter cards. Name one of the letters, and have each youngster show you the corresponding letter card. Hold up the appropriate teacher card to help students self-check their cards. Continue with the remaining letters. You'll be able to see at a glance which students recognize these letters.

Match My Letter

Give each student a few lowercase letter cards. Direct youngsters to spread out the cards on their tabletops or desktops so that the letters are clearly visible. Show students an uppercase letter card that corresponds with one of their letters. Have each child hold up the matching lowercase letter. Repeat with the remaining letters. Focus on different letters in another session.

All In A Line

Give each student a large letter card. If you have more than 26 students, assign some of them the job of Leader or Judge. If you have fewer than 26 students, some letters will not be used. In this case, at the end of the activity ask students to name the letters that weren't used, and have youngsters tell where these letters belong.

To play, have students arrange themselves in ABC order across the front of the room. After the students are lined up in order, have them hold the cards so that the letters are visible. Then, if you have a Judge, ask him to state whether or not he agrees with the letter sequence. If he disagrees, have him explain why. Help students make any necessary adjustments to correctly sequence the cards. Then ask Leaders to take turns using a pointer to direct attention to each card. As they do so, have each student who is holding a card name his letter.

Alphabet Art Activities

Young children love to explore and manipulate art materials. Channel that interest into these letter-related projects.

Play-Dough Letters

Use store-bought play dough or prepare homemade play dough in advance. (See recipe below.) Give each student a portion of the play dough. Provide time for students to explore it before beginning this teacher-directed activity. Have each child roll his play-dough into a worm shape. Then direct each youngster to form a designated letter with his play-dough worm. Hold up the corresponding letter card for students to use as a reference. Repeat with additional letters. For a fun variation, have students form and sequence the letters of their names.

Homemade Play Dough

Makes enough for approximately three to four students.

Ingredients:
1 cup flour
1/2 cup salt
2 teaspoons cream of tartar
1 cup water
1 teaspoon vegetable oil
food coloring, if desired

Directions:
Mix the dry ingredients. Then add the remaining ingredients and stir. In a heavy skillet, cook the mixture for two to three minutes, stirring frequently. Knead the dough until it becomes soft and smooth. Store the play dough in airtight containers when not in use.

Giant Letters

Have your young artists paint bigger-than-life letters. Provide classified ads or other newspaper sections for the backgrounds of the letters. Clip a sheet of newspaper to an easel. Ask a child to paint a large letter on the paper. Encourage him to fill the entire sheet with one giant letter. Remove the student's artwork to dry and prepare the easel for another youngster. Display the giant letters in ABC order in a hallway.

Letter Rubbings

Have each student select a sandpaper or glitter glue letter. (See page 55.) Direct him to place it on his desk. Then have each child place a sheet of duplicating paper atop the tactile letter. Instruct students to use crayons to rub across their papers. Letters will appear like magic!

Rainbow Names

Write each child's name on a separate sheet of duplicating paper. Make a copy of each and save the originals to use with this activity another time. Have each student use a crayon to trace the letters of his name. Encourage him to name the letters as he traces them. Ask students to trace their names several more times with different colors to achieve a rainbow effect.

Alphabet Art Activities

Sew-A-Letter Center

Use a permanent marker to print a large uppercase letter on a Styrofoam® tray. Poke holes along the letter outline approximately one inch apart. Cut a length of yarn and tightly wrap a piece of tape around one end to create a sturdy tip. Then thread the yarn through the first hole of the letter, leaving a tail that is approximately two inches long. Secure the tail to the back of the tray with tape. Have a student stitch along the letter outline. Prepare the card for another student's turn by unthreading the yarn to the first hole. Make additional Styrofoam® sewing cards as described for the remaining letters of the alphabet.

Make A Letter

Build letter associations by having students form letters with materials that begin with the corresponding letters. For example, have a student make a *B* with buttons or a *T* with toothpicks. Try some tasty letter projects, too, such as spreading jam on toast in a *J* shape or using Kix® cereal to form a *K*. The possibilities are limitless!

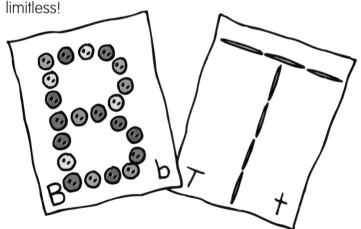

Alphabug

This curvy classroom critter is a creative ABC reference. To make an Alphabug, cut 27 large circles from brightly colored construction paper. Draw a face on one circle. Add antennae by taping black pipe cleaners to the back of the face. Give each child one of the remaining circles to use to make a body segment. Direct each student to tape short lengths of black pipe cleaners on the back of her circle for legs. Mount the Alphabug head on a bulletin board with the tape facing the wall. Help students add their circles in a curving line to create the Alphabug's body. Then print each letter of the alphabet on a separate body section in ABC order.

Variations:

- Use small paper plates instead of construction-paper circles. Attach the plates to one another with paper fasteners.

- Have students sponge-paint their circles. Allow the paint to dry. Then complete the project as described above.

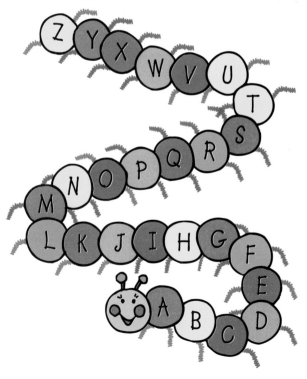

Students will love the fun-to-read alphabet rhymes on pages 63–75. Each playful rhyme is accompanied by a letter for tracing with a crayon and a picture for youngsters to color. Here are some of the many ways that you can use alpharhymes in your classroom.

Alpharhyme Books

To make individual alpharhyme books, duplicate a set of pages for each child. Cut the pages with a paper cutter and compile them in alphabetical order. Slip the pages inside a construction-paper cover. Staple the pages along the fold. Ask each student to personalize the cover of his book. After repeated readings at school, have each child take his book home to read with his family.

Alpharhyme Banner

Assign an alpharhyme to each child. If you have fewer than 26 students in your class, you will need to assign more than one alpharhyme to some youngsters. Have each student color his alpharhyme picture. Glue students' completed work in alphabetical order on a long sheet of bulletin-board paper. Display it on the classroom wall at students' eye level. Reread the rhymes together and provide pointers for students to use with the banner during center time.

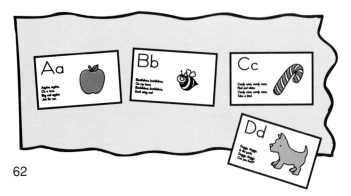

Alpharhyme Big Book

Copy each rhyme on a separate page of a small chart tablet. Either add your own illustrations or enlarge and cut out the pictures from the reproducible rhymes and glue them onto the tablet. Cover the front of the tablet with colorful Con-Tact® paper. Use a permanent marker to write the title "Our Alpharhyme Book." Read this book with students; then add it to your classroom library.

Use the alpharhyme big book for this shared reading activity. Ask students to predict how many times uppercase A is in the poem. Then have youngsters count the actual number as you read aloud the A alpharhyme with them. If desired, ask students to circle this letter each time it appears in the rhyme. Direct students to predict and count the number of lowercase a's in a similar manner. Then have students determine the total number of upper- and lowercase As. Repeat this exercise with other alpharhymes and the corresponding featured letters.

Skills Review

Here are some ways to review skills with alpharhymes.

After reading alpharhymes with students several times,

- have students identify the rhyming words.

- have students take turns using a pointer to count the number of words in each rhyme.

- ask youngsters to say, clap, and count the syllables or phonemes in each featured word (moon on the M page and popcorn on the P page, for example).

- select a word from a poem; segment the word and then ask students to blend the phonemes and say the word.

Alpharhymes

Illustrated by _____

- -

Listener Autographs

These people listened to me read this book:

63

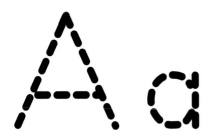

Apples, apples,
On a tree.
Big red apples
Just for me.

- -

Bumblebee, bumblebee,
On my knee;
Bumblebee, bumblebee,
Don't sting me!

C c

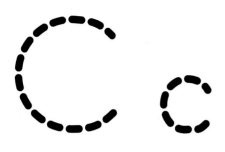

Candy cane, candy cane,
Red and white;
Candy cane, candy cane,
Take a bite!

- -

D d

Doggy, doggy,
In the park;
Doggy, doggy,
Can you bark?

E e

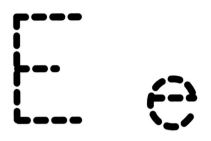

Eggs in a nest,
One, two, three;
Three baby birds
We will see.

F f

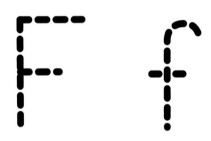

Fish, fish,
In the sea.
Fish, fish,
Swim to me.

Girls can run.
Girls can play.
Girls have fun
Every day.

- -

Hippo, hippo,
In the zoo;
Hippo, hippo,
Look at you.

I i

Ice cream, ice cream
In a cup;
Ice cream, ice cream,
Eat it up!

J j

Jam on toast,
Jam on toast;
That is what
I love the most.

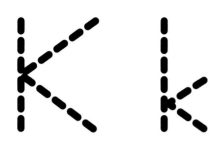

Kites fly high
In the sky.
See them go.
Blow, wind, blow.

- -

Lion, lion,
Can you roar?
Lion, lion,
Roar some more!

Moon so high
In the sky;
Make your light
And shine tonight.

- -

Noodles, noodles,
In a cup.
Noodles, noodles,
Slurp them up!

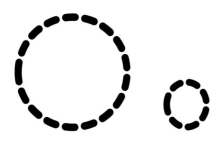

Octopus
In the sea;
Please do not
Swim near me!

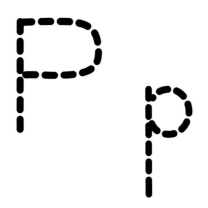

Popcorn, popcorn,
Pop, pop, pop;
Popcorn, popcorn,
Never stop.

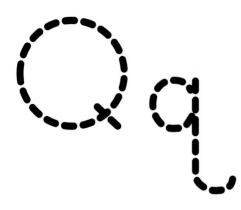

Queen in her castle,
Big, fancy house;
She hears "squeak, squeak";
Oh, no! A mouse!

Robin, robin,
In a tree;
Sing a song
Just for me.

S s

Seashells, seashells,
In the sand;
Pink and white shells
In my hand.

T t
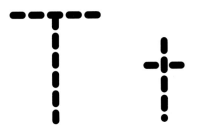

Tiny turtle
Likes to hide.
He tucks his head
Down inside.

U u

Under my umbrella
I am keeping dry.
Safe from the raindrops
Falling from the sky.

- -

V v

Vase of flowers,
Pink and red;
On the table,
By my bed.

Woodpecker, woodpecker,
Rap, rap, rap;
Woodpecker, woodpecker,
Tap, tap, tap.

- -

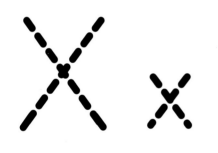

Look, look,
Can you see
X, Y, and
How about Z?

Letter-Sound Connections

Build students' ability to recognize and identify the beginning letters of words with these phonics activities.

Alphabet Blocks

Collect discarded tissue boxes to create large alphabet blocks. Write a letter on one side of a tissue box. Have students collect magazine pictures of objects that begin with that letter. Ask students to glue the pictures onto the box. Make additional blocks in a similar manner for the remaining letters of the alphabet.

Variation: Glue a different Alphapix (reproducibles on pages 78–84) onto each side of a small box. Use the cube to review beginning letters. Gather students in a circle. Gently toss the cube. Have students name the object on the top of the cube. Then ask the youngsters to isolate the initial sound and identify the beginning letter. Toss the cube again and continue as described.

Alphapix Letter-Sound Games

Reproduce the picture cards on pages 78–84. Mount them on tagboard and laminate. Cut the cards apart. Here are some of the many ways the picture cards can be used to review letter-picture associations and initial letter skills. (A certificate is also provided on page 84 for you to duplicate. Use it to recognize students' phonics achievements.)

- **Letter-Picture Memory Game**

  Write each letter of the alphabet on a separate card. For best results, make the cards the same size as the Alphapix cards. Shuffle the Alphapix and letter cards. Place all of the cards facedown in rows. (Place the letter-cards in rows separate from the Alphapix.) The goal of the game is to make the most pairs. A pair is made by matching a picture card with the corresponding beginning-letter card.

  To play, the first player turns over one Alphapix and one letter card. He names the object revealed and identifies its initial sound. The student also identifies the letter shown and the associated sound. If the cards make a pair, the player keeps the cards. If the cards do not match, the player turns the cards back over. Then the second player takes a turn in a similar manner. Play continues until all cards have been paired.

- **Find The Beginning Letter**

  Give each student a set of several Build-A-Word cards. (Reproducibles are on pages 12–16.) Ask students to spread out their cards on their tabletops or desktops so that each letter is visible. Show an Alphapix card that corresponds with one of the students' cards. Name the pictured object. Have students isolate the initial sound of the word and determine the beginning letter of the object. Then ask the children to hold up the corresponding letter card. Continue with additional pictures in a similar manner.

- **1, 2, 3; Look And See**

  For best results, conduct this phonics activity with a small group at a table or seated on the floor. Display several Alphapix cards. Tell students that you will name a letter. Youngsters will need to identify the pictured object that begins with the letter. To start the game, say, "1, 2, 3; look and see. *Show me something that begins with _____.*" After students determine the correct picture, remove that picture card from the group and add another card. Then scramble all of the picture cards and repeat the activity with different letters.

Letter-Sound Connections

Phonics Treasure Hunt

Try this jewel of a game to reinforce beginning-letter skills. In advance, determine how many and which letters you would like to use for this activity. Write each of the chosen letters on a separate cardboard box that is decorated to resemble a treasure chest. Review the sound associated with each letter. Then direct students to search for small objects that begin with the letters marked on the boxes. When a child finds such an object, have him place it in the corresponding box.

After the treasure hunt, gather students to look at their collective bounty. Select one box. Have students name the letter marked on the box and the corresponding sound. Then ask youngsters to name each object as you take it from the box. Repeat with the remaining boxes. Afterward, put all of the treasures into one unlabeled container. Have students use this container and the labeled treasure chests for an independent initial-letter-sorting activity.

To extend this activity, label a separate sheet of chart paper with each letter that was used. Record the names of the items in each treasure chest on the corresponding paper. Add simple illustrations. Post the lists in the room for ready reference.

Alphabet Soup

Place plastic or foam letters in a bowl. Stir the letters with a wooden spoon as you lead students in this chant: *"ABCs all in a group. What will I find in the alphabet soup?"* Have a student take one letter out of the bowl. Ask her to identify it and say a word that begins with that letter. Then direct her to return the letter to the bowl and stir all of the letters. Continue the activity until everyone has taken a turn.

Circle Of Sounds

Gather students in a circle. Say a letter, the corresponding sound, and a word that begins with that letter (*B, /b/, bat,* for example). Have the student to your left repeat the letter and sound. Then ask him to say a different word that begins with the same letter (*B, /b/, boy,* for instance). Next say another letter, the corresponding sound, and a word that begins with this letter. Ask the next student to your left to take a turn. Continue playing until all students have participated.

Beginning-Letter Sorting

Choose a letter for this activity. Collect several small objects that begin with this letter as well as several items that do not. Put all of the objects into a container. Place a Hula-Hoop® on the classroom floor. Place a card that is marked with the chosen letter inside the hoop. Seat students around the hoop. Have students name the letter on the card and identify the corresponding sound. Have students, one at a time, reach into the container and take an item. Ask each student to name the object and determine the beginning letter. If the beginning letter is the same as the letter in the hoop, direct the child to place the object inside the hoop. If it is not the same, have the youngster put the object on the floor outside the hoop. Continue until all of the items in the container have been placed inside or outside the hoop.

©1998 The Education Center, Inc.•*Phonics & Reading*—Grade K • TEC813

No "lion"!

_____ has done a g-r-r-eat job working with letters and sounds!

_____ _____
Teacher's Signature   Date

©1998 The Education Center, Inc.

High-Frequency Words

High-frequency words include regular as well as irregular words that do not follow phonics rules. With repeated exposure to these words in meaningful contexts, high-frequency words become part of a reader's sight-word vocabulary. The more words a reader identifies upon sight, the more fluently she is likely to read.

Students' names are wonderful high-frequency words to use for early reading experiences. These words have powerful meaning for students. Reading activities and materials that use students' own names and those of classmates can effectively teach many early reading skills.

Create a print-rich classroom environment of these high-frequency words. Clearly label children's coat hooks, cubbies, and other items with students' names. Also use job, attendance, and birthday displays during your daily routine to teach high-frequency words. Try these ideas to build students' reading vocabularies.

Activities That Use Names

Teacher, Teacher, Who Do You See?

The popular children's book *Brown Bear, Brown Bear, What Do You See?* written by Bill Martin, Jr., and illustrated by Eric Carle (Henry Holt And Company, Inc.; 1983) is a wonderful model for a whole-group pocket chart activity. After reading aloud this delightful predictable book, create a chart titled "Teacher, Teacher, Who Do You See?" Write the following text on sentence strips:
"_____, _____, who do you see?"
"I see _____ looking at me."
Insert cards with your name in the first two blanks and a student's name card in the third. (You might want to glue each child's photo onto his name card to provide a visual clue. Later in the year when students' sight-word vocabularies have increased, you might choose to eliminate the picture clues.) Have students read the chart with you. Continue with other students' names in a similar manner until everyone has taken a turn.

Name Puzzles

To make individual puzzles, write each student's name on a sheet of tagboard, leaving extra space between each letter. Make a dot below each letter. The dot will help students distinguish top from bottom when the letters are separated. Make puzzle cuts between each letter. Place each resulting name puzzle in an envelope that is labeled with the corresponding name. Have each student assemble his own name puzzle. Next direct students to return their puzzle pieces to their envelopes. Tell students to trade their puzzles with their classmates. Then ask students to assemble their classmates' puzzles.

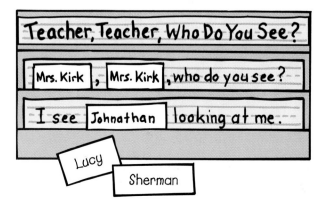

Nifty Name Card Activities

Geoff's Cubby

Chris' Coat Hook

Morgan's Cubby

Joel's Coat Hook

Sentence strips are convenient for creating name cards. One sentence strip can be used to create several name cards. Use a permanent marker to write as many first names as space allows on one strip. Cut the strip apart between each name. Make cards for last names with a different color of marker. Laminate the resulting name cards for durability. These name cards are bound to be one of your most-used classroom materials. Use the cards for these language arts activities.

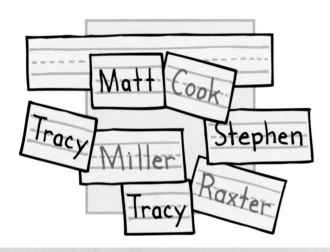

All Through The Alphabet

For an initial-letter review, list the letters of the alphabet from A to Z on chart paper. Give each student his name card. Have students whose first names begin with A come to the front of the group and show their cards to their classmates. Have students read the name cards together. Write these names next to A on the chart. Collect the A name cards and ask the children to return to their seats. Continue with the remaining letters. Read the completed chart with students. Then ask youngsters to count the number of names listed for each letter. Record the numbers beside the corresponding letters. Lead students to draw conclusions about the results.

Count The Letters

In advance, determine which student in your class has the longest name. Count the letters in his name. Prepare a chart that has at least that many columns. To begin the activity, give each student his name card. Have a student volunteer count the number of letters in his name and indicate the corresponding column on the chart. Write his name in this column and collect his card. Continue until all of the students' names are listed on the chart. Then help students count the total number of names in each column. Record the totals at the bottom of the chart as shown. To vary the activity, use last names.

All Sorts Of Names

Build a name graph with students to show how many parts (syllables) are in each of their names. To begin, give each student her name card and make several blank cards. Gather students in a large open area on the floor. Write "1" on a blank card to create a column heading. Set the card on the floor. Ask students whose names have one part to place their cards below the number card, forming a column. Then write "2" on another blank card to make a new column heading. Place it beside the "1" card. Have students with names that have two syllables arrange their name cards in a column below the appropriate heading. Continue in this manner until all students' name cards have been added to the graph. Then conduct a discussion about the graph.

More Nifty Name Card Activities

First And Last

For an interactive name-matching activity, arrange your youngsters' last-name cards on the chalkboard ledge. Ask a student to take his last-name card from the ledge. Then direct him to show this name card to his classmates and read it aloud. Give the child his first-name card and instruct him to place both his first- and last-name cards in a pocket chart. Then have him read his full name. Continue in a similar manner with the remaining students until all first- and last-name cards have been paired. Read the resulting class list with students.

Variations:

• Instead of using a pocket chart, have students match first- and last-name cards on a wall display, bulletin board, or clothesline.

• Conduct this activity with only half of your students' names at one time.

If Your Name…

To incorporate music into your phonics lessons, seat students in a circle on the floor. Have each student hold her first-name card. Lead students in this song, sung to the tune of "If You're Happy And You Know It":

If your name begins with A, begins with A,
If your name begins with A, begins with A,
If your name begins with A,
Then show us right away,
If your name begins with A, begins with A.

Have students whose names begin with A show the group their name cards. Then sing additional verses, substituting different letters. Modify lines if desired as well. For example, focus on final letters of names, or change the action in the fourth line.

Good Morning!

Gather students in a circle for a name review first thing in the morning. Hold all of your students' name cards in your hand. Lead students in this chant:

Good morning, good morning,
Good morning to you.
Good morning, _____.
How are you?

When you come to the end of the third line, hold up and read the first name card in the deck. Then finish the chant and have the named child respond to the question. Repeat the chant using a different name. Continue with additional verses until everyone has been greeted.

Spotlight On Students

Make each of your students a star for a day. Write each student's name on a slip of paper and place the slips in a brightly colored container labeled "Future Stars." Each day draw a name from the container to determine who is in the spotlight. Then conduct the activities described below.

Star-Studded Charts

Students will love to be featured in these charts. Each week, choose a topic such as "Things We Like At School." Write a related title on a large sheet of chart paper. Ask the student who is in the spotlight that day to share information about the topic. Write a sentence with this information on the chart. Have him add an illustration. Continue the chart in a like manner with the other students who are in the spotlight that week. Reread the chart with students each day before adding to it. If desired write students' names in a different color or circle the names. At the end of the week, post the chart at students' level. Have children practice reading it with a pointer.

"Star-iffic" Spelling

Write the name of the selected child on the chalkboard. Have students read it with you. Then direct students to clap and count the phonemes in the name. Ask students to identify and count the letters too. Have the child who is in the spotlight come to the front of the class. Ask him to select classmates to spell his name with letter cards. Help him distribute the appropriate teacher Build-A-Word cards to these students (reproducible on page 17). Afterward review the letters in the star student's name by asking youngsters to hold up specific letters.

If desired provide a set of name cards and student Build-A-Word cards at a center for youngsters to practice spelling classmates' names independently.

Topic Suggestions

- Pets
- Things We Like To Eat
- Our Favorite Toys
- Things We Like To Do
- Our Families
- Birthdays
- Things We Like To Wear
- Holidays
- After School
- Our Favorite Stuffed Animals
- Books We Like

Things We Like To Do

Grant likes math games.
Kyra likes to play ball.
Ramon likes to read.
Carrie likes to build with blocks.
Sarah likes to paint.

Our Favorite Toys

Sam likes his scooter.
Jessica likes her yo-yo.
Jason likes his skates.
Cindi likes her doll.
John likes his race cars.

Learning Names With Graphing Activities

High-interest graphing activities give children practice reading classmates' names. Graphing lessons also promote class discussions and reinforce a variety of concepts. Try these graphing exercises with your students.

Which Color Do You Like The Most?

7	red	Jen	Sam	Alice	Eva	Ben	Jack	Paul
5	blue	Sue	Jon	Tom	Beth	Ann		
3	yellow	Rick	Pam	Byron				

Color Our World

Use a paper cutter and three different colors of construction paper to make a class supply of small rectangles. Prepare a graph with three rows and several columns. Each resulting block needs to match the size of the paper rectangles. Title the graph "Which Color Do You Like The Most?" Glue a different color rectangle at the beginning of each row and write the corresponding color word on it. Next have students predict which of the three colors will be the class favorite. Tell each student to choose a rectangle that is the color he likes the most. Write his name on the rectangle. Direct each student to glue his rectangle in the appropriate space. After the graph is completed, count the total number of rectangles in each row. Record the number on the graph and lead students in a discussion about the results.

Birthday Time

Make a birthday graph on a large sheet of paper. Label it with the names of the months and write "What Is Your Birthday Month?" at the top. Write each student's name on a separate cake cutout. Write your name on a cutout as well. Display the cutouts in a pocket chart or on your chalkboard ledge. Ask each child to find the cake that is labeled with her name and have her take it to her seat.

Glue your birthday cake in the appropriate place on the graph. Direct students to add their cakes to the graph. Then conduct a discussion about the results.

Jason

Sample Questions For Discussion
What month has the most birthdays? The fewest?
How many more birthdays are in _____ than _____?
Who has a birthday in _____?
How many boys have a birthday in_____?
    Who are they? How about girls?

Have You Lost A Tooth?

Here's a great graphing activity to build name recognition and math skills, and get to know your students better at the same time! To prepare this activity, write each student's name on a separate wooden clothespin. Draw a line in the center of a sheet of poster board. Write "Yes" at the top of the left column. Draw a smiley face beside the word. Label the right column "No" and add a sad face. Write this question on a sentence strip: "Have you lost a tooth?" Display the poster board with the sentence strip above it. Have each student clip the clothespin with his name on the edge of the Yes or No column as appropriate. After everyone has had a turn, interpret the results with students.

This graph can also be used with other yes/no questions by changing the sentence strip. Ask students if they

- have a brother
- have a pet
- live in an apartment
- like pizza
- ride a bus to school

- have a sister
- live in a house
- live in a trailer
- like snow
- walk to school

The possibilities are endless!

Bubble Gum Words

To be proficient readers, students need to immediately recognize many high-frequency words. Students usually begin learning these words in earnest in first grade. Many high-frequency words are not phonetically regular and must be learned visually. To do so, students need repeated exposure to high-frequency words in context.

Start acquainting your kindergartners with high-frequency words with these ideas. Help students remember these words by calling them bubble gum words. Explain that bubble gum words stick all of the words together in sentences. Sentences would simply snap apart if they did not have bubble gum words to hold them together!

Bubble gum, bubble gum on my shoe. Bubble gum words stick just like glue.

Bubble Gum Word Cards

Using the list on page 91 as a reference, write each of the bubble gum words on a separate card. Cut around the configuration of each word as shown to help students form a visual memory of it. Then glue each of the words onto a piece of dark paper. Mount a simple picture of a large gumball machine on a bulletin board. Each time you introduce a bubble gum word to students, add the corresponding word card to the display.

Big-Book Bubbles

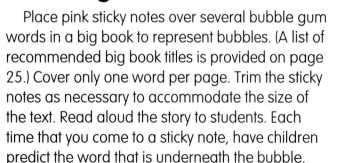

Place pink sticky notes over several bubble gum words in a big book to represent bubbles. (A list of recommended big book titles is provided on page 25.) Cover only one word per page. Trim the sticky notes as necessary to accommodate the size of the text. Read aloud the story to students. Each time that you come to a sticky note, have children predict the word that is underneath the bubble. Then remove the sticky note and read the word.

Bunches Of Bubbles

Highlight bubble gum words with a bubble-gum-pink marker that you use exclusively for this purpose. When you read charts and sentence strips with students, circle and color over the high-frequency words that have been introduced. The resulting pink bubbles will signal these important words to youngsters.

High-Frequency Word List

A
a
about
all
an
and
are
as
at

B
be
been
but
by

C
call
can
come
could

D
day
did
do
down

E
each

F
find
first
for
from

G
get
go

H
had
has
have
he
her
him
his
how

I
I
if
in
into
is
it

L
like
long
look

M
made
make
many
may
more
my

N
no
not
now

O
of
on
one
or
other
out
over

P
part

S
said
see
she
so
some

T
than
that
the
their
them
there
these
they
this
to
two

U
up
use

W
was
way
we
were
what
when
which
who
will
with
would
write

Y
you
your

Onsets And Rimes

Rather than applying phonics rules or sounding out words letter by letter, skilled readers look for patterns in words. This is called "decoding by analogy." Skilled readers compare patterns in unknown words with known words that have the same spelling pattern. For example, you can read the nonsense word "fay" because you already know the word "day", which has the same *ay* pattern.

Readers discover that vowel sounds are more reliable when they are part of a spelling pattern. Therefore, instead of teaching the short *a* sound in isolation, it is more effective if you teach it as part of a spelling pattern such as *at*. This approach is known as using *onsets* and *rimes*. The onset is the part of the syllable that comes before the vowel. The rime is everything after the vowel. In the word "cat," *c* is the onset and *at* is the rime. The rime is the predictable pattern.

There are 37 common rimes. Once readers are familiar with these rimes, they can read approximately 500 words (*Beginning To Read* by Marilyn Jager Adams, Massachusetts Institute of Technology, 1990, pp. 321–322).

Advanced kindergartners who are ready to start working with rimes should begin with those that have only two letters. First graders usually study rimes throughout the year.

Common Rimes

ack	ank	eat	ill	ock	ump
ail	ap	ell	in	oke	unk
ain	ash	est	ine	op	
ake	at	ice	ing	or	
ale	ate	ick	ink	ore	
ame	aw	ide	ip	uck	
an	ay	ight	ir	ug	

Word Families

Write a poem on a chart and read it with students. Choose a word from the poem that has a common two-letter word family (rime). Point to the word and have students identify it. Then focus on this word family for a word-building activity with the teacher Build-A-Word cards (reproducible on page 17).

To begin the activity, assign each letter of the selected word to a different student and give him the corresponding Build-A-Word Card. Have these students line up in front of the class to spell the word with the cards. Read the word with students and write it on the chalkboard. Direct the student who is holding the first letter to sit down. Give another student a different letter card to hold at the beginning of the word. Then ask students to say the new word. Continue making and reading additional words in a similar manner.

It's All In The Family

Create a row of houses for word family practice. To begin, draw and cut out a simple construction-paper house. Choose a rime and write it on the house as shown. Ask students to brainstorm words that have this rime. Record students' responses on a strip of paper. Underline the rime in each word. Glue the top of the list to the house and display the house at students' level. As you introduce more word families, make additional houses to create a neighborhood of rimes.

Word Family Book

For this small-group activity, write a rime on a sheet of chart paper. Ask students to brainstorm words that have this rime. Record the list of words on the paper. Have students help you underline the rime in each word. Add a simple picture clue beside each word. Write each word across the top of a large sheet of drawing paper. Assign each word to a student and have him illustrate it. Assist students in underlining the rimes. To make a cover, draw a house on another sheet of paper and add a title. Compile and bind the pages with the cover. Read the completed book with students, and add this handy word family resource to your library.

Tap, Spell, And Read

Use the Build-A-Word cards found on pages 12–17 and individual card holders (directions on page 11) for this hands-on activity. Choose a word family. Give each student the Build-A-Word cards needed to spell the selected word-family words. Have children sequence their letter cards in card holders to spell a specific word. Spell the word with the teacher Build-A-Word cards and display it for students' reference. Then instruct each child to tap a finger under each letter as he says the letter name aloud. Next direct him to slide his finger under all of the letters and blend the sounds to say the word. Have each youngster remove the initial letter of his word and substitute a designated letter; then continue the activity as directed.

What's Next?

By using the materials and participating in the activities described in this book, students
- learn about print;
- connect reading and writing in meaningful experiences;
- develop phonemic awareness;
- build phonics skills;
- increase recognition of high-frequency words; and
- begin learning about onsets and rimes.

While students build their phonemic awareness and phonics skills, you may want to think about what lies ahead for your youngsters. As you observe the range of reading and writing stages in your classroom, you'll see firsthand that the stages are not mutually exclusive. Students may exhibit skills at more than one stage at a time. Different educators label these stages in various ways, but the descriptions are generally similar.

Here is one overview of the development of reading skills.

The Stages Of Reading

1. Emergent	2. Beginning	3. Independent
The child	The child	The child
• reads using pictures and memory;	• demonstrates one-to-one word correspondence;	• uses a variety of word identification strategies;
• is aware of the conventions of print (He knows that text goes left to right, for example); and	• is starting to use phonics for decoding words; and	• reads fluently and with expression; and
• knows some letters and sounds.	• is developing a sight-word vocabulary.	• has a large sight-word vocabulary.

Undoubtedly the best way to help a child move from one stage to the next is to read with or to him every day. Youngsters also benefit greatly from reading aloud to adults. Sharing wonderful literature and your love of reading will have a significant impact on students' attitudes toward reading and their reading achievements.

The Stages Of Writing

1. Scribbling
The child writes with scribbles. His starting point may be anywhere on the page.

2. Directional Scribbling
The child scribbles from left to right, imitating adults' writing. He may add some letterlike formations as well.

3. Strings Of Letters
The child writes a series of letters with no regard to spacing. Upper and lowercase letters are mixed.

4. Letter Groups And Copying
The child groups letters to resemble words. He also copies environmental print. Reversals are common at this stage.

5. Letter/Word Representation
The child uses the first letter of the word and later, both the beginning and ending letters to represent entire words. For example, a child at this stage might write "I went to town" as "I W T TN."

6. Medial Letter Sounds And Sentence Writing
The child writes words representing beginning, middle, and ending letter sounds. He begins to construct sentences. For instance, a child at this stage might write "This candy is mine." as "This kande is min."

7. Conventional Spelling
The child spells most words accurately.

Give students lots of opportunities to practice writing, regardless of the stage at which they work. Praise their attempts. Model writing throughout the school day. As you do so, think aloud. Brainstorm story topics, talk about spacing between words, mention the need to go to the next line—in short, verbalize everything you do as you write. Model writing for a range of purposes, from writing attendance information on school office forms to writing newsletters to parents.

If you share the joy and purpose of reading and writing with students as well as help them develop the needed skills, students will be well on their way to becoming lifelong readers and writers.

Notes